The **Teacher's Essential Guide** Series

W9-CCZ-233

Jim Burke

Content Area Writing

How to:

- Design Effective Writing Assignments
- Teach Students Expository Writing
- Assess and Respond to Student Writing

SCHOLASTIC

Dedication:

To America's newest teachers

Series Editor: Lois Bridges

Development Editor: Dana Truby

Designer: Maria Lilja

Copy Editor: Chris Borris

Cover Photo: Bruce Forrester

Interior Photos: Noah Berger/AP and Jim Burke (where noted)

ISBN 13: 978-0-439-93447-3

ISBN 10: 0-439-93447-8

Printed in the U.S.A.

1 2 3 4 5 6 7 8 9 10   23   13 12 11 10 09 08

Contents

Introduction 4

Writing Instruction Self-Assessment 7

1. **Designing Effective Writing Assignments** 8

2. **Teaching Students to Generate Ideas** 22

3. **Teaching Students to Write Analytically** 36

4. **The Drafting and Revision Processes** 56

5. **The Polishing and Publishing Processes** 87

6. **Assessing Student Writing** 99

Recommended Resources and Readings 111

Introduction

"Writing is the largest orchestra your brain will ever have to conduct."

—Mel Levine

Writing is the most public performance of our intelligence. Students who struggle with reading can hide out, pretending they understand something they never read or choosing simply not to participate in the discussion of a text. Writing, however, is present—in black and white—for all to see. And what we see worries many in both education and business.

Approximately 50 percent of all entering freshmen fail the English Placement Test at California State University and end up in remedial writing courses. American businesses pay out roughly two billion dollars a year for remedial writing instruction for employees who lack the skills needed to write reports that are both coherent and correct. And even adults who don't need remediation often feel deep anxiety about formal writing.

With state exit exams and college placement tests such as the new SAT, we teachers now face increased scrutiny and pressure in the area of writing instruction. As Graham and Perin, the authors of *Writing Next*, note, "Along with reading comprehension, writing skill is a predictor of academic success and a basic requirement for participation in civic life and the global economy" (2007). Writing is, in short, essential to students' success in school, the workplace, and society at large. This book offers specific strategies to help us teach the skills and strategies students need if they are to achieve such success.

There are numerous aspects of writing instruction that intimidate teachers and often cause them to shy away from requiring students to write as often as they should. Many cite the time it takes not only to produce in-class writing but also to grade it. Others lack a sense of *how* to teach writing. The complexity of the writing process, which consists of both cognitive and emotional elements, can leave even the strongest teachers feeling ineffective, unsure of where to begin or how to proceed. Add to these anxieties the range of academic abilities represented in every class, each student with his or her own obstacles to becoming an effective writer.

Noah Berger

We need to know that there are techniques we can use to improve student writing and strategies we can employ to simply *get* them to write. This book focuses on both of these aspects of writing— learning to write and writing to learn, for they each make different demands on both the student and the teacher.

Students now enter a world that expects them to be able to write many types of documents using a range of media. They enter into an "attention economy" (Lanham 2006) in which their words and ideas must compete with others' if they are to succeed in delivering the intended message. They must be able to craft their message in 3,000 words, 300, 30, or, in some cases, none, using instead images and sound to say what words cannot capture. Such textual intelligence (Burke 2001) is the hallmark of modern literacy, which demands that students know how texts work so they can produce and read them effectively. One cannot develop such intelligence by osmosis; instead, it requires deliberate instruction. Writing is often *assigned*, but if students are to master this complex craft, it must be *taught*. This book is here to help you do just that.

Writing Instruction Self-Assessment

For each of the items below, record an answer between 1 and 5.

1 Never	2 Rarely	3 Sometimes	4 Usually	5 Always

- ☐ I design effective writing assignments and prompts.
- ☐ My students have no trouble generating ideas and details when writing.
- ☐ I teach my students to evaluate and analyze the effectiveness of their ideas and details.
- ☐ I teach students how to draft and revise their papers.
- ☐ I teach students strategies to polish their papers and provide opportunities for them to publish their papers.
- ☐ I effectively assess, respond to, and have students reflect on their papers.
- ☐ I teach students strategies for writing on demand.
- ☐ I teach students the elements of effective writing.
- ☐ Our school incorporates writing across the curriculum.
- ☐ I employ and teach students how to use computers and other technology to improve their writing.
- ☐ I have no trouble handling the paper load.
- ☐ I use a variety of strategies to support struggling writers
- ☐ I have no trouble with plagiarism in my class.
- ☐ I can effectively teach writing to large classes.
- ☐ I teach my students how to use writing to learn.
- ☐ My students are all motivated writers.

After completing this self-assessment, identify those areas with most urgent need of attention and improvement. For each statement to which your response was "never," "rarely," or "sometimes," go to the corresponding chapter and learn what you can do to improve in that area.

1. Designing Effective Writing Assignments

What students are writing about invariably affects how well they write. The assignment or prompt is the seed from which the writing will grow, watered either by tears of frustration or the sweat of inspired labor. Writing teacher Don Murray (2004) divides assignments into two categories: open and closed. "The closed assignment . . . has a clear educational purpose—the teacher and the students know what the assignment intends to teach" (94), while the "open" assignment "allows the student to be an authority on the subject," giving him or her the opportunity to create a topic and write in whatever form and style he or she choose. A closed assignment would be a traditional prompt that lays out the specific demands for the writer, something like, "Examine the effect of the Gold Rush on the culture of the West." The open assignment, however, would ask students to come up with their own topic on the Gold Rush, allowing, for example, the student with a passion for the environment to focus on the effect of various mining techniques. As Murray himself concedes, however, the open assignment is "more difficult when there is

Guiding Principles

- Make clear the purpose of the writing assignment.
- Make the assignment meaningful and challenging.
- Place each assignment within the larger context of your curriculum.
- Align each assignment with your state and district standards.
- Convey clearly the criteria for success on an assignment.

content to the course. When writing is taught as an adjunct to literature or when writing is used to test a student's knowledge of a subject, then the open assignment is more difficult" (99).

Let's face it: In some cases, we ourselves have no choice as to what our students will write about on exams for the state or the SAT. Such institutional topics are inevitable fixtures in today's instructional landscape. More often than not, they illustrate one or more of the qualities Edmund Farrell argues are *not* part of a good assignment. Farrell (in Connors & Glenn, 1999) says that a good assignment does *not*:

- Lead to an unfocused or too-short answer, such as "How do you feel about the ozone layer?"

- Pose too many questions in its attempt to elicit a specific response

- Ask students for too personal an answer, such as "Has there ever been a time in your life when you just couldn't go on?" or "What was the most exciting thing that ever happened to you?"

What *is* common to all good writing assignments, according to Farrell, is that they:

- Are meaningful to the students, though this does not necessarily mean the assignments are personal

- Are authentic, providing some context for writing that makes sense to the students; this does not mean they must always write a useful document such as a letter or an editorial, but it does mean that the writing should serve a purpose the students recognize as real

- Ask for writing about "specific and immediate situations rather than abstract and theoretical ones"

- Suggest a single major question to which the thesis statement of the essay is the answer

- Help students practice specific stylistic and organizational skills

Here, then, are some guidelines for designing writing assignments and prompts:

Make clear the purpose of the writing assignment.

When you have students write, no doubt you do so with a specific purpose in mind. A social studies teacher might want them to show how one event led to another, or to contrast two cultures, leaders, or periods. For English teachers, writing assignments often involve responding to or interpreting other texts, though if you are teaching composition, the assignment might well call for a persuasive essay as part of a larger unit on argument. Whatever the subject, a good assignment requires clearly stated outcomes, all of which should be written out (instead of spoken or jotted down on the board). Here are some suggestions to keep in mind when designing an assignment:

Determine and clearly state the purpose of the assignment. Will students: analyze, compare/contrast, define, describe, evaluate, persuade, explain, and/or summarize? Take time to have students underline and discuss these words and their implications for writing. Focus on just one or a few of these skills with each assignment.

Specify the requirements of the assignment in writing.
These might include all or some of the following:

- Genre (e.g., essay, letter, opinion piece)
- Length
- Deadline
- Documentation (e.g., works cited, bibliography)
- Steps (e.g., brainstorm ideas, outline, draft)
- Assessment criteria
- Introduction
- Directions
- Standards addressed by this assignment
- Requirements (e.g., number of texts they must refer to in their research paper, amount of data they must include in their analysis)

Identifying the standards for any given assignment is, in some districts, a requirement; for others, it is simply a useful part of the planning process, one that assures you are teaching your students the lessons the state expects them to learn.

Take time to discuss the assignment with your students, going over key words that signal which strategy to use (e.g., analyze, define, persuade, contrast). In addition to taking time to discuss the assignment, be sure they know what they must do and what a successful performance on this assignment will look like.

Here is a sample assignment, one I created for my freshman class at the end of a unit on our relationship with the natural world.

Our Relationship With the Natural World Writing Assignment

Standards

This assignment addresses California Language Arts standard 2.3: Write expository compositions that marshal evidence in support of a thesis and related claims, including information on all relevant perspectives, and convey information and ideas from primary and secondary sources accurately and coherently.

Topic

Compare and contrast the different types of relationships humans have with the natural world. Include examples from your own experience and the different texts we have read or viewed. After comparing and contrasting, make a claim about what you feel are our rights and responsibilities toward the natural world in general. Provide reasons and evidence to support your claim.

Requirements

2- to 3-page typed paper, double-spaced, with appropriate headings and bibliography. Must include examples and quotations from at least three texts

Deadline and Evaluation

Rough draft is due Wednesday; final draft is due the following Wednesday. Your paper will be evaluated according to the criteria outlined on the attached rubric.

Make the assignment meaningful and challenging.

While common sense suggests that assignments related to students' interests would inspire hard work and better writing, this is not always the case. In recent years I have seen the following topics on district writing assessments, no doubt selected because of their connection to students' interests:

- Write a letter to the principal explaining why students should or should not be allowed to have cell phones at school.

- Write an essay in which you argue for or against school uniforms.

- Write an essay for or against video games, explaining why you think they are or are not beneficial to those who play them.

Clearly these topics relate to and interest kids. Yet as someone who had to sit all day in a cold room with other teachers and read these essays, I found the topics resulted in writing that tended toward ranting as opposed to effective argument. The fact that the essays, despite all the emphasis on their importance, had no consequence and received no grade further undermined any investment in the writing. What should we do, then, to ensure that our students are motivated and able to write well on our assignments? Following are some suggestions:

Consider all the possible forms that might be appropriate for this writing assignment. Options might include essays, letters, op-eds, narratives, Web sites, speeches, summaries, and research papers. Other possibilities exist, of course, but as our focus here is academic writing, we will not examine those.

Jim Burke

Ensure the assignment is meaningful by connecting it to students' experience. This does not necessarily imply the assignment has to delve into students' personal lives, but it does recognize that students have a limited range of experiences to draw on based on their age and circumstances. Often we assume they have learned about subjects or had experiences they have not and are thus not prepared to write about. The social studies teacher can surely ask students to write about a particular invention from the Industrial Age that revolutionized the world but may engage her students and get better writing (and thinking) if she asks them to compare that Industrial Age invention with one from the present and then to explain how the modern invention will have a similar effect on the economy, culture, or people.

Look for or create authentic opportunities to write for purposes that motivate students. My students, over the years, have written biographies of centenarians for a local hospital, letters to officials, and speeches that they later delivered before audiences made up not only of classmates but the mayor, superintendent, and other local leaders. They cannot always be writing for real audiences like these, but when they can, they should. After I took my freshmen to visit the University of California at Berkeley, for example, they wrote formal letters in which they reflected on what they learned, discussed what impressed them, and thanked the program director for arranging the visit. These letters, which we sent, were later used by the program director to show the value of her program and ensure its continued funding.

Make room for students' own voices in the assignments whenever possible. They understand that you have to teach them certain academic forms, but this does not necessarily mean they cannot write in ways that express their own ideas. Regardless of what subject you teach, think of the great writers in your field and the distinct voices they bring to their writing: E. O. Wilson (science), Garry Wills (politics), David McCullough (history), Keith Devlin (math), and many others, of course. Making room for students' own voices means making room for them in the assignment, and this increases the likelihood of greater engagement.

Place each assignment within the larger context of your curriculum.

Each assignment is, or should be, part of a larger sequence appropriate to your subject. Such sequencing is crucial, as some assignments demand much more than others. An assignment should require skills students already have or those you will be able to effectively teach within the context of that assignment. The following are a few recommendations to follow when planning a sequence or creating an assignment:

Consider the cognitive demands of each assignment in light of the overall goals of your course. We traditionally divide writing into four modes: narration, description, exposition, and argumentation, often assigning them to different grade levels, though, in truth, students should be working in these different modes constantly. The first two, narration and description, tend to be easier for students because these modes are based on more concrete material: events they personally experienced or things they have observed and can describe. As assignments become more abstract, they often become more difficult to write about.

Arrange assignments in order of difficulty, using each assignment to teach those skills that will prepare them for the next. Teaching students how to summarize on one assignment will give them the skills they need when asked later to insert quotations and summaries of other sources as part of a larger paper with a more challenging goal.

Embed within each assignment those smaller but no less important skills your students need to achieve the course objectives. Good writing assignments inevitably integrate within them a series of smaller writing opportunities, each of which allows you to teach such skills as summarizing, taking notes, responding to an idea, and paraphrasing another's argument as you formulate your own.

Noah Berger

Keep in mind the important connection between writing, reading, and speaking, all three of which complement one other. Each writing assignment provides rich opportunities to focus on these other areas throughout the assignment. Rarely will any instructional sequence allow you to focus on only one of these three fundamental literacies, so the instructional sequence must ensure that students are taught the necessary skills at each step.

Align each assignment with your state and district standards.

Almost every state in the country has adopted standards for just about every subject area. Most, if not all, of those standards include requirements for writing appropriate to that subject area. Some districts have adapted the state standards to their own local needs, culling out and emphasizing what are often called "power standards." Such power standards are those standards the department emphasizes but which are still part of the required state framework. Here are a few representative examples:

Physical Science: Interpret, display, analyze, and draw conclusions from the results of a scientific investigation.

English/Language Arts: Compose a written message/ statement utilizing the correct format to focus writing for audience and purpose.

Social Studies: Compare and contrast different cultures in terms of family, social class, religion, education, arts, and other aspects of daily life.

Here are a few strategies to use when designing your own assignments:

- Consult your state and district standards to identify those standards which are a natural part of the assignment you are creating. Include the standards on your assignment handout to identify to your students those goals central to the assignment. You do not have to list them all, nor must you use the bureaucratic language of the state. Notice that on my sample assignment on page 12, I list only one standard and, because they form a useful checklist, the subpoints, as well.

- Use the academic language appropriate to these standards to ensure that students learn it. In my freshman English class, for example, we take time to study the specific terms of argument (e.g., claim, reason, evidence, rebuttal) as we learn and practice them within the larger context of an assignment that calls for them to write an op-ed piece for or against the existence of zoos in the wake of a recent occurrence in which a tiger escaped from its enclosure.

- Integrate the standards into your assessment criteria. One measure of your instructional effectiveness should be that students have made progress toward or mastered the standard.

Convey clearly the criteria for success on an assignment.

As you begin to design assignments, you must always have the end result in mind. Know what the criteria are by which you will measure it. Such criteria also help to anchor your instruction and direct your use of class time: Is this activity or lesson related to the goal? Will it lead the students to success on this assignment? If not, rethink your assignment.

Ericka Lindemann's (2001) "Heuristic for Designing Writing Assignments" is very helpful for determining appropriate criteria. Lindemann recommends asking yourself the following questions as you plan.

1. **What do I want the students to do?** Is it worth doing? Why? What will the assignment tell me about what they've learned? How does it fit my objectives at this point in the course? Does the assignment assess what students can *do* or what they *know*? Am I relating their work to the real world (including academic settings) or only to my class? Does the assignment require specialized knowledge? Does it appeal to the interests and experiences of my students?

2. **How do I want them to do the assignment?** Are students working alone or together? In what ways will they practice prewriting, writing, and rewriting? Are writing, reading, speaking, and listening reinforcing one another? Have I given students enough information to make effective choices about the subject, purpose, form, and mode?

3. **For whom are students writing?** Who is the audience? Do students have enough information to assume a role with respect to the audience? Is the role meaningful?

4. **When will students do the assignment?** How does the assignment relate to what comes before and after it in the course? How much time in and outside of class will students need for prewriting, writing, and rewriting? To what extent will I guide the students' work? What kinds of help can students constructively offer one another? What deadlines do I want to set for collecting the students' papers (or various stages of the project)?

5. **What will I do with the assignment?** How will I evaluate the work? What constitutes a "successful" response to the assignment? Will other students or the writer have a say in evaluating the paper? What problems did I encounter when I responded to this assignment? How can I improve the assignment? (221)

The following suggestions offer some ideas about how to establish and communicate the criteria for a successful performance on any given writing assignment:

- Clearly list the criteria for success on the handout and clarify these criteria, explaining the terms as you go.

- Provide examples from the textbook or past student papers to show students what a successful performance looks like on this assignment. If, for example, one requirement is a clear and compelling claim, provide students with samples to illustrate what such a claim looks like.

- Revisit the criteria throughout the writing process. Make each criterion the focus of a mini-lesson to help students keep it fresh in their minds.

2. Teaching Students to Generate Ideas

All students occasionally struggle to get started on a writing assignment. Some struggle continuously. They may not engage with the assignment or it might ask them to write on a subject about which they know nothing. Or they may simply struggle, as John Steinbeck often did, to discover what to say and how to say it: "It is strange how this goes on. The struggle to get started. Terrible. It always happens. I am afraid." Here Steinbeck recognizes what studies consistently emphasize: the internal obstacles to writing. Mark Twain compared writing to sending a bucket down into the well. When the bucket came up empty he knew it was time to get out into the world, usually by traveling on a steamboat down the Mississippi, to replenish his supply of stories. You can't take your students down the Mississippi, but you can use the same strategies writers have developed over the years. And you can provide the supportive environment needed to take the risks and explore the possibilities that good writing requires.

Mel Levine (2003) confronts the difficulty some students have with getting what is inside of them *out* onto the page, calling it the "myth of laziness." Levine redefines this problem as "output failure," something most students experience.

In my AP English Literature class, for example, all students feel overwhelmed by the challenge of writing about *Hamlet*, lacking the strategies they need to generate more complex ideas and find textual evidence to support those arguments; however, in my English class, these less experienced writers, many of whom have identified learning difficulties, lack more fundamental strategies for writing even about more familiar, concrete subjects, such as their own experiences. These troubles have greater consequences than in the past due to increased pressure from state tests, which now include writing assessments about typically dull topics students must discuss in a thoughtful essay written in 20 minutes, often incorporating details from an accompanying expository article they must first read.

Noah Berger

Generating ideas is a little like making sausage: It's a messy process that requires you to grind ideas to make the final product palatable. Inexperienced writers often neglect this important stage, throwing down whatever comes to mind to get the assignment over with, while more experienced and advanced writers spend as much as half their writing time actually thinking, grappling with ideas, organizing structures, arguments, and details for the assignment they must write. If students are to become consistently effective writers, however, they must learn a range of strategies they can use to generate such material, especially when they struggle to get anything out at all. This chapter offers you specific techniques you can teach students so they can get their great ideas out of their head and onto the page.

Guiding Principles

- Have students read to learn new ideas about the subject.

- Have students write to discover what they know and need to learn about their topic.

- Talk through the prewriting process to generate and elaborate on ideas.

- Ask questions to create new associations and deepen initial thinking.

- Observe models, procedures, productions, and performances.

- Have students use graphic organizers to stimulate ideas and make connections.

- Provide critical thinking strategies to help students articulate ideas.

Have students read to learn new ideas about the subject.

Ask students to read a particular text with the purpose in mind of generating ideas for the paper they must write. If, for example, you want students to write a paper on the connection between food and health, have students read a range of texts, taking notes as they read newspaper articles and textbooks and view documentaries and Web sites. In such cases, students are using these texts not to study but to gather information about the subject. To get ideas for this chapter, for example, I read many books and articles on the writing process, taking notes as I read, just as in my English class students read sample personal narratives to give them ideas—about style and content—for the narratives they will write themselves.

Have students write to discover what they know and need to learn about their topic.

Writing to think or gather ideas can take several forms. Teach all these different techniques, allowing individual students eventually to choose which strategy works best for their thinking style. Free writing involves writing nonstop about the subject for a specified period of time and then sifting through that material for key ideas and interesting connections. Journaling, while similar to free writing, asks students to write informally about ideas or questions you provide, all of which are chosen for their ability to stimulate thinking related to the assignment. Other techniques include taking notes while reading or listening, listing ideas and possible titles, brainstorming and clustering ideas for a more visual way of generating ideas, and making connections before and during writing. In truth, I often use several of these approaches, beginning perhaps by asking students to write a list of associations, statements, titles, whatever ideas come to mind. Once they have generated some rough material, I will ask them to choose *one* idea from their list and then do a free write in

Jim Burke

their notebooks for five or 10 minutes, after which I might, time allowing, ask them to reread what they wrote and underline those few ideas that rise to the top and show some potential. My next step might be to send them home with those ideas to do some more generative reading (or rereading) of relevant texts, and write a very sketchy outline for the next day.

Talk through the prewriting process to generate and elaborate on ideas.

Discussion is inherently generative, especially when combined with other strategies such as asking questions, observing, or reading. It is often useful to have students talk about the assignment and what they might say about it, taking notes as they do. For example, if I have students use a graphic organizer to generate ideas for their paper, I will usually have them work together to complete it, discussing their ideas as they work; or if they complete it on their own, I might then have them use that organizer as the basis for a discussion, the purpose of which is to add more details to and refine their own ideas on the topic at hand. Also, if students read a text or observe something (e.g., a video, a process, a performance), I will have them discuss it and ask them, during this conversation, to take notes on the key elements that they might use in the paper they need to write. In my freshman English class, for example, students were writing an essay on Odysseus's journey. To prepare them, we first discussed what the elements of a journey were by using a clip from *The Lord of the Rings*, which I repeatedly interrupted, asking them to turn to a partner and analyze the film. After further discussion, they had a working model of the journey cycle they could use for their paper. Throughout the writing process, of course, they continued to discuss how each step of the cycle applied to *The Odyssey*.

Ask questions to create new associations and deepen initial thinking.

Questions are the most important tools the writer has. When we write, there is always a question at the heart of the work, one we are trying to answer. I often begin an assignment by asking the class, "What are the questions we should ask to help us think about this topic?" For many students this is a new experience and they can find it difficult, wanting the teacher to "just give the answers." Yet few strategies help more than learning to ask questions to stimulate thinking and evaluate the

> QUESTIONS TO ASK: POETRY
> 1. Who's the speaker?
> 2. What's the occasion?
> 3. What's the subject?
> 4. What's the poets' (sp) purpose/point?
> 5. What strategies/devices does poet to achieve this purpose/point?

importance of what they have begun to gather. While this is a helpful beginning, other questions such as these have traditionally helped writers:

The Reporter's Questions: Who, what, where, when, why, how—and "So what?"

Classical Topics: What is it? (Definition) What is it like? (Analogy) What is the consequence? (Cause-Effect) What do the experts say? (Testimony)

Four Core Questions: What goes with what? (Association) What opposes/resists what? (Opposition)

What follows what? (Progression) What changes into what? (Transformation)

Analytical Questions: What is it made of? What type is it? What is the relationship between x and y? How are a and b similar and different?

These are familiar and proven question sets, but each topic tends to suggest its own questions, those that will help unlock the ideas and potential within both the writer and the topic itself. In my freshman English class, my students write about a person who was an "ally" during a difficult or important phase of their lives. I give students three questions to help them generate and organize their ideas:

Problem: What was the problem or difficult experience this person helped you get through?

Solution: How did they help you get through this experience?

Consequences: What effect did this person's actions have on you after it was over?

Before students use these questions for their own writing, they use them as reading tools as they analyze several models I have them read and annotate, labeling specific passages with these terms.

Observe models, procedures, productions, and performances.

Whether a movie or a science experiment, visual media can help make the abstract more concrete. Sarah Galvin, who teaches freshman English, showed a student-made documentary from YouTube.com on the Little Rock Nine as part of a unit on equality and inequality in communities. Instead of just having them passively watch, however, she gave them a graphic organizer, which they used to identify key details and then sort them into four categories. Next, Ms. Galvin extended these categories to connect this material to Steinbeck's *Of Mice and Men*, thus

allowing the students to generate a much more analytical reading of the story. A graphic organizer (see page 32) then served as the basis for the writing assignment, providing structure and support for the class discussion and writing that followed.

This last point is important: Observation should involve other generative strategies—discussion, writing, taking notes, reading—to complete the generative transaction and thus prepare the student for the writing assignment. Observing can also include examining models of the assignment. Whenever possible I give the class an example of the kind of writing that I want them to do, presenting it on the overhead and giving them a copy to annotate. We think aloud about what the text does that makes it effective. These observations often suggest an organizational structure to the student. For example, observing a scientific procedure, a student may realize it has a cause-effect pattern or a chronological one. Such patterns are themselves useful generative techniques as the students begin to think about, "Okay, what should go first? And now second? And so on."

Have students use graphic organizers to stimulate ideas and make connections.

Graphic organizers offer powerful support for writers of all levels, providing a structure that helps students not only generate ideas but also identify connections between those ideas. I use them most often to help students in the initial phase of the writing process. The first step is to ask what kind of thinking you want the students to do and which tool might best support their efforts. A simple target, for example, can get students thinking about a topic. Write the topic (e.g., Industrial Age Inventions) in the center and then have eight different major discoveries in the inner circle. Students can then elaborate on each discovery in the spaces on the outer circle. This prewriting strategy lends itself to collaboration by allowing students to compare their results in small-group discussions, or you can use a whiteboard or transparency as a means of facilitating a full-class discussion. Use graphic organizers as a tool to generate and refine ideas, or pose questions.

Graphic organizers are useful when students read. A good graphic organizer helps students to sort their ideas and thoughts into creative material for subsequent writing assignments. Again, the key step is to ask what kind of thinking you want students to do and help them choose the tools that will facilitate such analysis.

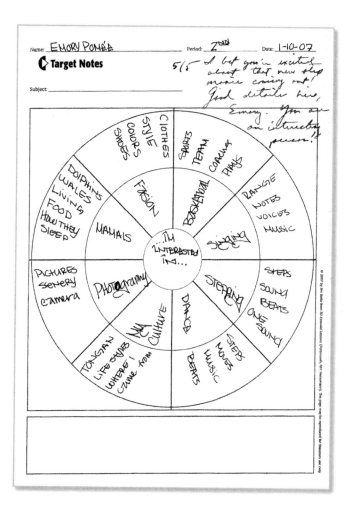

In my freshman English class, I asked students to read a collection of stories and essays that explored the essential question, "What does it take to be a survivor?" I created Survival Notes for them to use while reading. We used the graphic organizer as a basis for group and class discussions, all of which prepared them to write an essay on the traits of survivors.

Survival Notes

The character survives by being...	For example, he...	This helps him survive because...

Provide critical thinking strategies to help students find and articulate writing ideas.

Often, students need structural support to generate and communicate their ideas. The language of critical analysis is difficult to acquire for some students, especially when they are reading texts that are new and difficult for them to understand. Creating lists on the board or posters on the wall with strategic sentence starters can help students begin the process of developing their initial ideas into language they can refine as they move through the writing process.

Sentence Structures: Helping Students Discuss, Read and Write About Texts

SENTENCE STARTERS
Making Predictions
I predict that...
If *x* happens, then...
Because *x* did *y*, I expect *z*.
Making Connections
X reminds me of...
X is similar to *y* because...
X is important to *y* because...
Summarizing
The main idea is...
The author argues that...
In _____, (author's name) implies...
Synthesizing
These elements/details, when considered together, suggest...
Initial impressions suggested *x*, but after learning _____ it is now clear that...
It is not a question of *x* but rather of *y* because...

SENTENCE FRAMES

Responding

X claims _____ which I agree/disagree with because...

X's point assumes y, which I would argue means...

While I agree that_____, you could also say...

Agreeing

Most will agree that...

I agree with those who suggest that...

X offers an effective explanation of why y happens, which is especially useful because most think that...

Disagreeing

I would challenge x's point about y, arguing instead...

X claims y, but recent discoveries show this is...

While x suggests y, this cannot be true since...

Arguing

Although x is increasing/decreasing, it is not y but z that is the cause...

While x is true, I would argue y because of z.

X was, in the past, the most important factor, but y has changed, making it the real cause.

A related approach is to give students strong statements on the board, overhead, or a handout—to respond to, in order to start the fire of discussion, such as:

- Video games are not a waste of time but a way of improving your mind. (English)

- We are *all* Hamlet. (Literature)

- The Great Depression was not a curse but, ultimately, a blessing. (Social Studies)

- Junk food should be outlawed in schools. (Health)

In response to such statements, students might choose from a list of sentence starters such as these:

- I agree that _____ but not that _____ because . . .

- X is true because . . .

- Some people think _____ about x, but I/others say _____ because . . .

No one prewriting method is perfect for all students. Instead, consider each strategy in light of your students' learning style and your specific assignments. At the heart of these suggestions, however, is the idea that writing requires not only a culture of support and inquiry but also the time and encouragement to fully engage in that inquiry. I am reminded of a cartoon I saw some years ago: A man reclines in a cabana on the beach, staring off through the window while a sign on the door warns: "Do Not Disturb—Writer at Work." We may not be able to provide the cabana or the beach, but we can—and should—provide students the time and opportunity writers need to think before they write. Given the different schedules all teachers have and the competing demands we struggle to meet in a given semester, it's hard to say what is enough time, but we should not expect good or engaged writing if we rush to get it done, making what should be a meaningful learning experience simply another assignment to check off as completed.

3. Teaching Students to Write Analytically

When students have finished all that gathering and generating, they have little more than a big pan full of mud that may or may not have nuggets of gold hidden in it. To find the treasure, they need to analyze what they have discovered and determine how it fits in with their topic and writing task. How long this process takes depends, of course, on the time students have: If it's a timed writing, such as a state exam, they might have 30 minutes to generate, evaluate, analyze—and *write*! If, on the other hand, they are writing a process or research paper, they have more time for this stage.

Students must determine which of these details are relevant and most effective as they move from concrete, familiar writing territory (e.g., description, personal narrative) to more abstract, complex assignments (e.g., compare and contrast *a* and *b*, or use your data to explain how *x* causes *y* and discuss the implications). This stage is crucial to an insightful, effective piece of writing, for it is here that the writer begins to weave all these ideas together prior to actually putting them into paragraphs of what will become the paper they must write. Here, the writer makes important decisions such as what her subject will be and what she will try to say about it, what form all this should take, and which details are most important to her purpose or the argument she will develop about this subject.

Though there are many complex stages to this process of evaluation and analysis, teaching your students a few key principles can help them to steer their way through the writing maze.

Guiding Principles

- Help students break down the writing task.

- Help students develop a focus for analysis.

- Teach students how to choose the evidence or examples that suit their writing purpose.

- Teach students how to organize their ideas prior to writing.

- Show students how to synthesize their ideas and plans as they begin to write.

Help students break down the writing task.

Writing prompts come in all shapes and sizes, some clearer and more interesting than others. While you might create thoughtful, engaging writing assignments for them, your students are still likely to encounter vague or bland topics on standardized writing tests. If you teach your students how to approach any writing task, they are likely to be more successful and write with greater insight. Of course, you may choose not to give prompts, but instead simply offer topics with a loose set of constraints. Such an assignment might ask students to "write about how the character changes over the course of the story," or "compare a society from the past with one from the present and explain how they are similar." What's important is that students learn how to attack writing prompts and compose an effective response.

- Identify the key words in the prompt. Focus on the verbs that say what you *must do* and the nouns that spell out what your essay *must include*. Here is a sample prompt from a Modern World History class; note the verbs and nouns which have been singled out:

> Write <u>an essay</u> in which you <u>identify</u> <u>one key discovery from</u>
> <u>the Industrial Revolution</u> and <u>formulate</u> <u>an argument</u> about
> its importance. In this essay, <u>describe</u> <u>the invention</u> and
> <u>explain</u> <u>how it benefited society</u> not only then but continues
> to help us today. Include in your essay <u>relevant examples</u>
> <u>that support and illustrate your assertion</u>.

- Deconstruct the prompt with the class. Ask your students to underline the key words. Then, walk through the assignment line by line and ask students to share what they've noticed. Discuss key points as you go. Be sure to remind them to underline such key words in all writing prompts, especially timed essay exams.

- Teach students to evaluate all their possible options. Push them to find several ways they could respond to this topic from the generative stage, and choose the one that is most compelling.

- Ask students to determine which ideas, evidence, or other details they have so far that are appropriate and valuable to this prompt.

- Show students how to turn a writing assignment into a checklist of what the writer must do in his or her essay. This is useful on any writing assignment but especially so on a timed writing test. Failing to fully answer the prompt is consistently cited as one of the main reasons for a lowered score on the Advanced Placement English and state writing exams.

Assessment Vocabulary

(Adapted from Kate Kinsella's *Common Academic Writing Tasks*)

Analyze   Break the subject (an object, event, or concept) down into parts, and explain the various parts.

Critique   Point out both the good and bad points of something.

Define   Give an accurate meaning of a term with enough detail to show that you really understand it.

Describe   Write about the subject so that the reader can easily visualize it; tell how it looks or happened, including how, who, where, why.

Evaluate   Give your opinion of the value of the subject; discuss its good and bad points, strengths and weaknesses.

Explain   Give the meaning of something; give facts and details that make the idea easy to understand.

Interpret   Explain the meaning of a reading selection; discuss the results or the effects of something.

Persuade   Give reasons in order to get someone to do or believe something; appeal to the reader's feelings and mind.

Respond   State your overall reaction to the content, then support your individual opinions with specific reasons and examples, making sure to refer back to the reading.

Summarize   Briefly cover the main points; use a paragraph form and don't include any personal opinions about the content.

Help students develop a focus for analysis.

Your goal at this stage is to help students learn how to bring their subject into focus, as a photographer brings an image into focus with the lens. Murray (2003) calls this the "focal point," saying

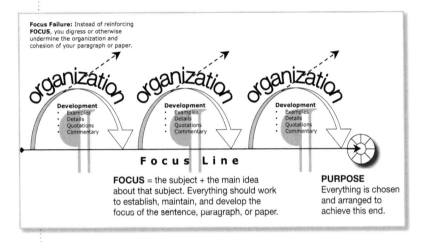

Focus Failure: Instead of reinforcing **FOCUS**, you digress or otherwise undermine the organization and cohesion of your paragraph or paper.

organization   organization   organization

Development
- Examples
- Details
- Quotations
- Commentary

Development
- Examples
- Details
- Quotations
- Commentary

Development
- Examples
- Details
- Quotations
- Commentary

F o c u s   L i n e

FOCUS = the subject + the main idea about that subject. Everything should work to establish, maintain, and develop the focus of the sentence, paragraph, or paper.

PURPOSE
Everything is chosen and arranged to achieve this end.

that when the writer finds this point it "energizes" the writing by, in part, showing how all the ideas and the topic can be tied together.

I ask writers to think about the focus of their paper as the spine that runs through its body. To help them further refine their focus into a a thesis statement, we use these strategies:

- State the problem embedded in the text of the writing assignment. For example, when my freshmen wrote about their "allies," those who had helped them through a difficult time, I asked them to state the problem and explain *briefly* how this person helped them solve it. This was not meant to be a rough draft but merely a quick effort to move them closer to a main idea about their subject. One student wrote, "My problem was that my grades were going down and I needed discipline. My uncle helped me by giving me discipline and making me do all my homework and reading. He was also there to guide me when we had just moved to the United States."

Have students ask themselves:

- Do I have enough specific, accurate INFORMATION to build a piece of writing that will satisfy the reader?

- Does the information focus on a single, significant MEANING?

- Do I see an ORDER in the material that will deliver the information to readers when they need it?

- Do I know readers who NEED the information I have to give them?

- Do I hear a VOICE that is strong enough to speak directly to the reader? (57)

Adapted from Donald Murray (2004).

These questions can be rephrased for younger students or used singly. The point is to develop in your students the ability to evaluate the value of their material, the viability of their ideas, and their readiness to begin actually writing.

- Post useful questions on the board or on a poster for easy reference. Young writers must learn to internalize these questions as part of their own individual composing process, making them habits of mind.

  - What is the subject of my paper?

  - What is the point or argument about this subject?

  - Who is the audience for this paper?

  - Why is my argument important? (or, So what? and Who cares?)

  - What details are most relevant and compelling to my main idea?

- What is my attitude toward this subject?

- What does the reader already know or feel about this subject?

- What do I want readers to know, understand, or do when they finish reading my paper?

- What genre or form is most appropriate for this topic?

- What does the prompt say I must do or include?

- What are the criteria on which this paper will be assessed?

- Use a graphic organizer to discover or refine the focus of the paper at right. An organizer like the Conversational Roundtable asks students to place a subject or main idea at the center and then begin analyzing which category each detail might be sorted into, while also determining, informally at this point, how they relate to the main idea.

Conversational Roundtable

Topic _____

Suggestions for use: Ask yourself what is the focus of your paper, discussion, or inquiry. Is it a character, a theme, an idea, a country, a trend, or a place? Then examine it from four different perspectives or identify four different aspects of the topic. Once you have identified the four areas, find and list any appropriate quotations, examples, evidence, or details.

- Have students shape it into a working thesis. Students must transform an idea into a topic and, finally, into a thesis their paper will explore, explain, or persuade the reader to accept as a reasonable argument based on the evidence they provide. A *topic* would be, for example, the invention of the automobile, the importance of sleep in adolescent development, or the use of language in Conrad's *Heart of Darkness*. As Booth, Colomb, and Williams (2003) suggest, "a topic is usually too broad if you can state it in four or five words" (43). Such broad topics not only make it difficult to achieve a coherent focus throughout the paper but overwhelm the writer who must gather the details and evidence to write about such a large topic. Put the general topic on the board and ask students to practice revising it into a more focused version. For example, "the invention of the automobile" could become, "the impact of the invention of the automobile on American culture." The challenge now is to take this emerging topic and shape it into an argument that is neither too broad nor too narrow and which the students have the evidence to support. On the board, I then take the topic and work with them to transform it into a working claim. First, I have them write their own claim based on the more refined topic, and then we discuss what they come up with. I often write some of theirs on the board, then revise one or two of these into a stronger version. Thus we have a three-step strategy for developing a working thesis:

Step 1: Generate topic

Example: The invention of the automobile

Step 2: Refine topic

Example: The impact of the invention of the automobile on American culture

Step 3: Change topic into a working thesis

Example: With the possible exception of the personal computer, no other invention has transformed American culture as the automobile has.

I should add, returning to an earlier strategy, that writers can easily turn this thesis into a question they can use to evaluate and guide them along the focus line to their stated purpose. Here, for example, is a set of questions I put up on the overhead and used to help my seniors refine and revise their focus on a paper about Conrad's *Heart of Darkness*, as they were trapped at rather obvious, surface-level thinking. I put it on the overhead, uncovering it step by step as I had them answer the same questions about their own essays, which we then discussed.

Refining and Revising Your Essay's Focus

1. What is the subject of your paper?

2. What is the question your paper is trying to answer?

3. On a scale of 1-10, how important is this question?

4. Why is this question important? That is: So what? (Revise your question to be more meaningful.)

5. What is your new claim?

Asking students to reflect on their writing process offers clues into kids' writing experience and, at the same time, what works to keep them writing. One of my students writes:

> The process by which I wrote this paper was just continual rumination and revision of different ideas. I have found that I am a lot better off and that the writing comes more easily if I choose a topic that actually interests me. In delving deeper into the essay, I realized that asking the question, "So what?" works wonders, although I could probably have asked it even more often while writing this essay.

Teach students how to choose the evidence or examples that suit their writing purpose.

Once students have this working focus line to follow, they must return to what they generated and begin evaluating the capacity of the details to help them prove their point. In some cases, students will first need to do more research into their topic, using the strategies outlined in the previous chapter, now that they know the point they are trying to make. To return to a previous example, students in my class had to write about an ally of theirs. After first generating a list of all the people they considered allies, students had to choose one to focus on; one of my freshmen, Sonia, chose the mother of her childhood friend who helped her through a difficult period. Sonia stated the problem as "not having a stable home and not seeing my mom and dad a lot. They were always working and going through a divorce." In response to the question, "How did this person help you solve the problem," Sonia wrote, "This person helped me solve it by letting me go to her house and she would take care of me. I could sleep over at her house and I would be welcome. She had a safe environment for me." By framing the topic as a problem, Sonia creates a useful means of deciding which of the details she generated are useful for her essay. I had students use the Narrative Notes organizer to first generate more details (in the Notes column) and then move toward some initial organization to the paper in preparation for writing a draft. Other strategies, such as the rhetorical modes listed below, help students to further refine their focus even as they are choosing the details and evidence for their essay before or as they begin to write.

Narrative Notes

Focus: Nariman & Nadia

Second Mom
Sister I never had
Taught me a lot
Took care of me from when I was 6 months until 11 years old
Went to my birthday parties
Had four kids

Beginning

Met through a friend
Went to her house almost everyday
Her daughter Nadia was a few years older than me

Middle

Taught me how to tie my shoes and other life skills
Played with Nadia every time I was at Nariman's
Great family

End

Still keep in touch
Five kids now
Miss them a lot

Sonia's example suggests the following strategies are useful for this stage of the process:

- Ask students to restate or consider their topic as a problem instead of a thesis. Using the earlier example about automobiles, I might come up with the problem of transporting people and products in a timely manner. By recasting my thesis as a problem, I can examine it from different sides and choose the examples, details, quotations, evidence, and data that will help me do that. Dombek and Herndon (2004) suggest asking students to write a letter to a friend or family member about a problem they have not been able to solve. In the letter, which can be written at several different points during the process, students should try to get the other person to see there is a problem and to consider it from the writer's perspective, offering a range of ways to address or resolve it. This kind of embedded exercise allows teachers to focus on the thinking writers must learn to do if their writing is to be clear and effective.

- Ask the students to select the details, examples, and quotations based on their ability to add substance to their paper. Many writers, especially those writing five-paragraph essays, choose examples that are all of one type and rarely advance the topic or ask the reader (or writer, for that matter) to consider the topic from other sides. Thus your students should choose—and do some more generating if necessary—examples and quotations that represent points of view that contradict or challenge elements of your argument, or suggest possible exceptions. The point here is to remind students to use these other perspectives on their topics to clarify and strengthen their own ideas by showing that their students know and have already thought through others' ideas.

- Revisit your purpose in light of the prompt itself and rhetorical modes listed in the table below:

Rhetorical Mode	Answers the Question
Narrative	What happened and when?
Definition	What is it?
Classification/Division	What kind is it? or What are its parts?
Process Analysis	How did it happen?
Cause and Effect	What caused this to happen?
Argumentation/Persuasion	What do I want the reader to think, believe, or do?
Comparison/Contrast	How is x similar to or different from y?
Example/Illustration	What is an example of x?

- Ask your students questions to help them evaluate and analyze the different materials they have gathered in light of their audience, purpose, and main idea. Here are some sample questions you can list on the board or in a handout for students to ask themselves at this or subsequent stages of their composition process:

  - What interests or surprises me most?

  - Which idea(s) can I write about best under the circumstances of this assignment?

  - Which one invites or makes best use of the details and ideas I have gathered?

  - What will everyone else writing this assignment say about this subject?

- Given that most will write about *x*, what is a compelling but different angle I might adopt for this subject?

- What detail, image, fact, or idea is most memorable, most important, of those I have gathered so far?

These questions are helpful in all writing situations as each writer is trying to develop a voice and a stance on a subject that will distinguish him or her from the others. As one who has graded district and state essays, I can tell you that they all quickly blur into one mediocre voice, periodically interrupted by a few writers who dared to make the prompt their own and write against the grain of all the others.

Teach students how to organize their ideas prior to writing.

As students move closer to actually writing, they must assess their ideas and focus, and find an organizing principle. The traditional five-paragraph essay would call for three main qualities or ideas about this topic, but such a structure inevitably leads to writing that lacks vigor and depth since the writer must move on to the next idea just as he or she is beginning to scratch beneath the surface. The organizational capacity I am speaking of is more subtle, but is evident when students approach the subject as a question or a problem. Help your students understand that they can use one or more of the following approaches to assess or develop the organizational structure of their paper before or as they begin to write it:

- Integrate into your instruction these specific organizational principles that are most appropriate to the prompt or point students are trying to make. This might mean providing samples that show students how such information might be organized by different patterns (e.g., compare/contrast vs. classification) or teaching them specific organizational patterns.

- Ask students to use a particular graphic organizer, such as a Venn diagram, to help them give shape to their ideas and thus, in this case, improve the comparison.

- Use a variation on graphic organizers such as the technique of clustering. This approach helps students identify the different categories into which they could sort their ideas and then gives them a means of evaluating whether the details and data they have will actually sort out into these categories. In this process, students can begin to evaluate and analyze the relationship between the categories and details, determining which are most important and which show the most potential as they begin to write.

- Show students how to outline their ideas using a range of strategies that include flexible, informal outlines. Try to avoid the formal numerical and alphabetical systems that sometimes hinder thought at these early stages when students are still trying to discover

Organizational Patterns

1. **Sequential**
   Arranged in the order that events occur. Also known as *time order* or *chronological order.*

2. **Geographical**
   Arranged according to location or geographic order.

3. **Classification**
   Organized into categories or groups according to various traits.

4. **Listing**
   Arranged in a list with no consideration of other qualities.

5. **Cause-Effect**
   Arranged to show connections between a result and the events that preceded it. Similar to *problem-solution.*

6. **Order of Importance**
   Organized in order of importance, value, or some other quality.

7. **Compare-Contrast**
   Organized to emphasize similarities and differences.

the organizational structure of their ideas. Only later, when they are writing or have a solid working draft, can students begin to organize their ideas with some greater rhetorical purpose in mind.

Show students how to synthesize their ideas and plans as they begin to write.

At this point, some students are ready to be turned loose to get down that initial draft; most, however, need to better understand what they have to say and how it all fits together. Others have yet to arrive at any clear idea about what they intend to say and need to corral all their ideas into the shelter of a controlling idea; otherwise their essay will end up resembling a typical President Coolidge speech, which I heard described once as a pack of wild horses breaking free across the plains in need of a firm hand to bring them under control. Here are some ideas for teaching students how to make these connections so they arrive at the next stage of the process knowing where they want to go and how they might get there:

- Have students write what Donald Murray called a "discovery draft," which he defined as "more of a late predraft . . . that the writer pushes on to the end, no matter if there are holes and parts of the writing that clearly do not work [but that allow] the writer . . . to work with a completed whole" (2004 51). It is in this discovery draft that writers can assess what they know—or need to know. Such a draft—which I often refer to as a "down draft," meaning to just get something down on paper to work with—further assesses the viability of the subject and the writer's perspective on it, the structure and the reader's needs. In short, such a draft marks the transition from thinking to writing about a subject. While it may evolve into a working and, ultimately, a final draft, it is more of a rehearsal, something like the way actors block a scene before running through it and beginning to master it. True, many students these days prefer to compose directly on the computer, yet the purpose here is still to explore their thinking, not to get the assignment done, which is often the concern for those students. I will use one of several strategies to help students write such a discovery draft:

- Have your students write a timed in-class version to get them thinking about the subject by writing in more of a structured form instead of taking notes and doing generative free writes.

- Send students home with all their notes and ideas, which they may have discussed in class that day as preparation, to write a discovery draft, usually with the suggestion that they take no more than an hour.

- Ask students to do a free write, which is a variation on the discovery draft, the goal of which is more generative, less focused on creating a whole draft of the assignment the student must write. It is a method, usually applied in class, for gathering and connecting what students have so far, but one that also helps them begin to find their voice, their stance for the subsequent drafts. When I use this technique, I ask them to write anything they have to say about the topic for a given period of time (e.g., 10–15 minutes).

- Assign students to groups to discuss their ideas so they can synthesize what they think at this point. Think of these discussions as editorial meetings common to all publications: Everyone sits around the table pitching ideas to colleagues who challenge the writer with questions designed to clarify. During such meetings, all writers should take notes they can use later when they write their drafts.

- Require students to write an actual rough draft of their introduction and first body paragraph. This method

Jim Burke

forces them to stand (well, okay, *sit*) and deliver a concrete beginning, to commit themselves, through language and their stance, to the writing. I ask them to write only the intro and first paragraph because, like the foundation of a house (in which all their ideas will live), this beginning gives a clear sense of where they are going and how they think they will get there. In a variation on this approach, one I will use if explicitly teaching students to write introductions, I have them write three different introductions, each using a distinctly different voice and stance. Then students share these with peers the next day, asking them to identify which one is most effective and why. The writer then chooses, based on that feedback, the best introduction and formally begins the draft.

- Have students write a proposal in which they summarize their ideas and what they will say in the paper. This approach is especially helpful for larger projects, such as research papers, as it puts writers in the position of having to advocate for ideas they must begin to refine, to shape into an argument they can present. If they are still struggling, it will be clear; such struggles will clarify your next steps. In such a proposal, which Donald Murray calls a "query," the writer lays out the topic and what she will say about it, but also explains why the idea and the perspective on it are important, as well as how she will develop the idea. Some suggest writing this proposal as a letter to the teacher, putting the student in the position most writers occupy when they must write to a publisher to pitch an idea for an article or a book.

- Require students to create a PowerPoint presentation to frame their ideas prior to writing them into the assigned form. This does not require going to the computer lab, though such a trip does provide a useful context in which to teach students how to use such software; instead, they can use a storyboard organizer to sketch out their paper on a "paper PowerPoint." While this technique is less useful for narrative writing, it is perfectly suited to both expository and academic writing, which have specific points that support an overriding argument. Whether students discuss or even present these ideas depends on your instructional goals and the time you have. Students in my AP literature class, for example, must analyze *Hamlet* according to a particular theory of literature (e.g., Marxist, feminist, psychoanalytical). Before writing the actual paper, they work in groups to research the subject and collaborate on a formal presentation using PowerPoint. When they finish these presentations, they will have read, discussed, and presented their ideas, all of which have prepared them to then write the paper, for which they now have a detailed outline in the form of their PowerPoint slides as well as an emerging fluency on the subject thanks to their presentation before the class.

4. The Drafting and Revision Processes

I did not understand the notion of drafting and revising until I wrote my first serious piece of public writing: my wedding vows. My then-fiance and I, a couple of young 24-year-olds just returned from living abroad (she in Japan, I in North Africa), opened a bottle of wine and sat down at our shiny new computer. We had brainstormed and gathered ideas from others' vows, including the traditional ones. As soon as we started in, one of us would question the other, saying, "Well why *not* say 'forever after,'" or some such hairsplitting query. As we worked through the evening (and the wine), a draft emerged, one we could work with, one we could shape into what would become the final draft after many versions.

One can only commit to such a process, however, when one genuinely cares about the subject at hand. A state writing test a few years back asked students to read an informational article on and then write an expository essay about hummingbirds. All across the state kids were sitting down to think and find something compelling to say about—that's right—hummingbirds. You can imagine the results. Students often must write about remote topics on class and state exams, and do so under the pressure of time, which allows no chance to draft and revise. In such cases the first draft must show the potential for a great final draft that they will never get the chance to write.

When it comes to getting a draft down on paper, we need to give students permission to write terrible first drafts. Students are often not used to actually working through the process of a paper, so they tend to want to get it down and call it done. It falls to us, as their teachers, to create not only a process but a culture in which they can work as real writers, trying out and leaving behind ideas in a process that is not really linear but rather more dynamic and interactive. It is important to ask students to reflect on their writing process, or certain aspects of it as they work on it. After writing, one of my students reflected:

> "I started out with a horrible first draft. Lately, for some reason, I am never happy with what I initially write. I have to go back, write, and rewrite a point. It is frustrating, but for some reason or another, that is what my writing has come to. I think that maybe this just means I am growing as a writer."

The reflections of one of my freshman students remind us that we must teach students how to get that first draft down and how to revise:

> "The process of writing this took up lot of time, but also gave me the chance to remember things that I have forgotten. My progress as a writer has greatly improved now that I have been taught how to revise. Before this semester I didn't know how to revise at all. Now that I know the strategies you have taught us my essay writing will continue to improve."

Guiding Principles

- Provide guidance to help students learn to draft and revise.

- Embed writing instruction throughout the drafting and revision process.

- Have students evaluate and revise their writing based on needs and insights.

- Create opportunities for feedback throughout the drafting and revision process.

Provide guidance to help students learn to draft and revise.

As college graduates, we have years, even decades, of experience writing academic papers about topics we may or may not care about. We have paid our dues. I remember one freshman composition class I had in college in which I received a C- on the first five papers I wrote. A psychology paper came back dripping with red ink, the most memorable line on it being, "You're not writing a short story here, Mr. Burke. This is a scientific paper." Somehow I found the courage to go into these professors' offices and ask for help, saying in essence, "I don't know what you want. Show me what a successful paper looks like." And they did, so I improved, slowly but surely.

Middle and high school students need similar support, though we don't have the leisure of office hours (or an office!) to meet with and discuss the papers of our 150 or more students. What you need is a way to provide such support to whole classes or individuals through groups as they draft and revise their papers. Here are some representative examples of what you can do to help students draft and revise their paper for your class:

- Provide a range of models so students know what a successful performance on an assignment looks like. Such examples can come from your students, from state and AP exams, or professional writers, as well as textbooks. The following example, which I created for my freshman English class, had goals: helping students to improve their introduction writing and how to elaborate on their ideas with more detail. I first put it on the overhead, covering up Version B. I then asked them to generate questions about Version A, all of which I wrote on the board. After revealing and discussing what made Version B more effective, I had them apply the same questioning strategy to their own papers. Note that this sequence helped them simultaneously draft and revise their essay. Here is the sample I wrote:

Version A: *Death at the River*	Version B: *Death at the River*
The world beyond my stretch of Keane Drive was unknown, uncharted. All we knew was that beyond it lay dangers we had heard of. None of these dangers came to mind, however, that summer day when John Russell rode up and asked if I wanted to go for a ride. Unwilling to show my fear, I straightened up and said, "Sure, let's go." And so we headed off, two 10-year-old boys in cutoffs.	The world beyond my stretch of Keane Drive was unknown, uncharted. All we knew was that beyond it lay dangers we had heard of: big streets with fast cars driven by crazy teenagers, strangers who would take us away, and, of course, the river, which was filled with not only rushing waters but stories of the lost lives my father spoke of when telling me of his own childhood. None of these dangers came to mind, however, that summer day when John Russell rode up on his bike and asked if I wanted to ride along the new bike trail at the river. Unwilling to show my fear, I straightened up and said, "Sure, let's go," though a small quiver in my voice no doubt betrayed me, as it did when I called out the lie to my mother a minute later: "Mom, John and I are going for a ride over to his house to play some basketball." And so we headed off, two 10-year-old boys in cutoffs, our pale chests bared to the hot summer sun of Sacramento, unaware that behind the bright light of the day hid a darkness which that day would reveal to us through events we would never forget.

As we discuss Version A as a class, I ask my students which elements of the writing need to be developed. So it goes: sentence by sentence, generating questions to help me revise my initial draft. Once all these questions are written up on the board, they read Version B, underlining any additions they notice as they read.

Together we rewrite it, until we have a piece of writing similar to Version B. Now they are prepared to apply the same technique to their own papers, so they trade and write such questions in the margin, then revise to add the details their reader said are lacking.

Tech Note! You will find a rich collection of sample essays, prompts, and rubrics on state and federal departments of education Web sites as well as on the College Board Web site for the Advanced Placement exams. Some states as well as the College Board provide sample papers scored with commentary to help teachers and students better understand the nature of an effective paper.

- Offer students a range of support at the sentence, paragraph, and paper level. Students often struggle to find the language to say what they know or what sounds like the samples you have offered. Each genre of writing or type of essay makes its own demands. While this type of guidance will help some as they draft, most will not be able to consider this type of help until they are revising. The different sentence structures in the sample essay help students see how they can say certain things more clearly, with greater power, especially when working with complex ideas. For example, I will call their attention to the "Summarizing" section (p. 33) when students must read and summarize an article, providing related examples to help them further see what I am after. When working with more advanced assignments, such as "Disagreeing" (p. 34), I will write these sentence

Maria Lilja

frames on the board and model for them how to apply these: "I would challenge Achebe's point about Conrad's racist attitudes, arguing instead that he agrees with Achebe and uses the narrator to point out the racist ideas of the Europeans in Africa." Once I have modeled this for them, students must then use the same structures to write or revise their own statements as they develop or refine their arguments.

- Use examples during both the drafting and revising processes but for specific purposes. Sometimes you might be working on how to write more effective introductions or conclusions to a paper; on other occasions, such as the example below, you might be teaching them to develop their ideas through the use of examples and commentary, something students find particularly difficult as they move into more academic writing. The following example offers a good way of how to do this, but to make it clear let me describe the steps first:

  1. Students were writing a short paper that synthesized the ideas from multiple readings, in this case about the role of allies in our lives.

2. Students read and annotated three articles about people and the role allies had played in their lives.

3. Students then wrote a paragraph that was supposed to have a clear focus, effective organization, and good development in the form of examples and commentary.

4. After students wrote their first paragraph (see Sample A), I created a sample of the same assignment rich in the details I found lacking in theirs. I arranged this in an outline form to help them see better how I organized and developed my ideas and printed it to an overhead transparency.

5. I then put this example on the overhead projector and led them through it, pointing out what I did, how I did it, and why.

6. They used my example to help them revise their first draft, the improved version of which you can see in Sample B, written by the same student in my freshman class.

Sample A (Sara's first attempt)

All three of these people had challenges and obstacles that presented themselves to them throughout their lives. And all three of them had certain allies that helped, supported, and encouraged them along the way. People that they themselves even said that they wouldn't have been able to do it without. It's important to have people on your side and rooting for you, sometimes it makes all the difference in the world.

Here is my sample paragraph, full of the details I wanted them to include in their own essays, arranged into outline form as I presented it to them on the overhead first, before giving them a copy to study and use:

My Example

- People find guidance from so many different people, some of whom are obvious allies, while others are unexpected.

  - Yet it is not who these people are that matters as much as what they do to help us accomplish our goals.

    - One thing they do, perhaps the most important, is believe in us.

    - Kelly Zimmerman Lane, for example, came from a house filled with the alcoholic violence of her father; yet her mother and grandmother protected her from this abuse, showing her through their example that they expected her to accomplish great things.

      - As she said, "Success... was the only option."

    - Actor Mario Lopez also had parents who supported his interest in drama, coming to every performance and signing him up for any class he wanted to take.

    - Not everyone has parents who can help them, though.

      - Reverend "Monk" Malloy, former president of Notre Dame, lacked "any models in [his] family for going on to college," but found in Sister Eleanor a mentor who took a special interest in him early on.

        - Malloy, like the others, benefited from his ally's high expectations.

          - * For example, Sister Eleanor "gave [him] a tremendous amount of confidence, exposed [him] to the thrill of learning, and convinced [him] that [he] had a moral obligation to use the opportunities available to [him]."

  - One way or another, each of these allies taught Lopez, Lane, and Malloy that, as Lopez says, they had "to be focused and disciplined," that they had to have "dedication, strong will, and mental toughness," all of which their allies helped them develop.

Here is Sara's revised version, written after we discussed my model:

Sample B (Sara's second attempt)

Everyone has allies that help them in different ways to accomplish something. All three of these people had challenges and obstacles that presented themselves to them throughout their lives, and all three of them had certain allies that helped, supported, and encouraged them along the way. People that they themselves said that they wouldn't have been able to do it without. For Kelly Lane, it was her mother and grandmother who were her biggest allies after her father left the picture. Her grandma took her and her sister in, and her mother set the ultimate example of success for Kelly. For Mario Lopez, he had his dancing, wrestling, and drama coaches to set examples for him and guide him. And finally, Reverend "Monk" Malloy, had Sister Eleanor, his teacher for three years in a row. She inspired him and made him like school even more. It is important to have such people on your side rooting for you because they can make all the difference in the world.

Some teachers might worry that by providing a model students are just copying what you do, a reasonable concern. I would say only that the apprenticeship method has served us well for centuries. The process of mimicry, combined with the gradual move toward independence, gives students the support they need at the level they need it. Thus I provide some form of differentiated instruction, telling the class to use as much of my model as helps them complete the assignment without using my exact words, for it is often the sentence structures and organizational patterns they are learning.

Embed writing instruction throughout the drafting and revising process.

When examining effective literacy instruction, Langer (1999) found that teachers incorporated strategies into their instruction so students developed independence; a second major finding of such instruction was that students learned skills and knowledge through a range of lesson types. After all, we cannot learn by mini-lesson alone. The key to such embedded instruction is that it is situated within the context of students' learning and therefore provides a more responsive, targeted form of teaching that helps students learn the lesson at hand, or prepares them for those problems on the horizon. If, for example, I am teaching students to write a persuasive essay, I am simultaneously creating a perfect opportunity to teach them what a claim is, a topic well suited to a short lesson which they can then apply to their own paper while we work on them in class. If they show an acceptable level of mastery, we can then move on to the reason for their arguments, doing still more mini-lessons on how to state these reasons, or provide the evidence that best supports their claim, and so on.

The basic structure of such mini-lessons is pretty straightforward and should take anywhere from 10 to 30 minutes depending on the complexity of the material:

1. Identify the subject of the lesson (e.g., writing effective introductions)

2. Provide the rationale for the lesson, connecting it to the paper they are writing.

3. Go over the lesson in detail, providing examples to illustrate your main points.

4. Provide time for students to take notes and ask questions for clarification on the topic of the mini-lesson.

5. Ask students to practice the lesson at that time through some commercial materials or those you create yourself.

6. Discuss problems students had or questions that arose during the practice.

7. Have students apply what they learned to the paper or other assignment they are actually working on and for which this lesson was the reason.

In her study on effective literacy instruction, Langer identified three types of instruction: *separate* instruction, during which discrete lessons are taught (steps 1–4 above); *simulated* instruction, during which students have the opportunity to practice the lesson and gain initial understanding (steps 5–6); and, finally, *integrated* instruction, during which the students apply the content of the lesson to the paper on which they are currently working (step 7).

While I sometimes use the whiteboard or project material using an LCD projector attached to my laptop, most of the time such lessons take place with me at the overhead projector, pen in hand as I present and we discuss the lesson at hand. The overhead allows me to structure the lesson with their needs and the time in mind, since I have only a 50-minute period. What follows are some representative examples of lessons I have used with my classes:

- Summarize key points about the topic or lesson to provide succinct delivery and promote effective note-taking. Here is a sample overhead I created for a lesson on effective introductions:

Effective Introductions

- Establish the focus by introducing the subject, narrowing it down, and making a statement (claim, thesis statement) about the subject.

- The thesis statement usually appears near or at the end of the introductory paragraph. It is the main point you will try to prove.

- Use one of the following strategies for an effective introduction:

  - Begin with an intriguing quotation or series of quotations.

  - Ask a question or pose a series of questions about the subject.

  - Define the subject (though avoid the overly familiar "According to *American Heritage Dictionary* a crime is a...").

  - Make an unexpected or compelling comparison.

  - Open with a controversial statement that challenges but does not offend or distract from the point you want to make.

  - Tell a relevant but engaging anecdote.

  - Draw the reader in with the promise of new insights or information about a subject that interests him.

  - Establish your credibility as a writer through a combination of *what* you say and *how* you say it.

  - Set up some sense of structure so the reader knows how information will be organized and can read it effectively.

New Teacher Note Creating such handouts in your own voice for your students is one of the best ways to learn your subject in greater detail. Such handouts have been, for me, a form of personal professional development. What's more, they allow me to adapt them to the assignment and class I am teaching and thus make me more effective.

Here is a more specific lesson, this one on how to incorporate quotations effectively into an expository paper. This particular sample was created by my colleague Sarah Galvin. I include here the handout as an example of such a lesson and explain how she had students use it.

Jim Burke

Sarah gives students their own copies of this sheet, puts a transparency of the same document on the overhead, then asks students to get out different color highlighters. After going over the reason for using quotations and discussing the sandwich diagram, she has them highlight the words that lead up to or introduce the quotation with one color, use a second color to highlight the quotation itself, and use still a third color to indicate the commentary on the quotation. After ensuring that her students understand the lesson, she has them use the highlighters on their own papers. For those who cannot identify any lead or commentary for their quotation, she has them revise the paper to add these elements.

Quote Sandwich

Properly using quotes is more than just rewriting it from a text. To be effective, you need to surround the quote with **support** and **explanations**. Think about it like this: Use quotes to prove a point or support an idea, not to show that you have read the story.

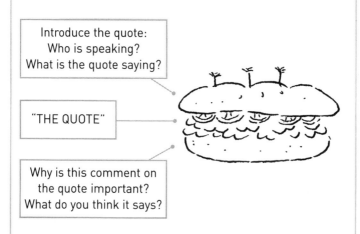

Introduce the quote:
Who is speaking?
What is the quote saying?

"THE QUOTE"

Why is this comment on the quote important? What do you think it says?

Sample quote from *To Kill a Mocking Bird by Harper Lee*: "You never really understand a person until you consider things from his point of view. . . until you climb into his skin and walk around in it."

Atticus gives Scout a crucial piece of moral advice that governs her development throughout the novel. He implies it is easy to pass judgment on others, but one cannot fully understand another's character unless they have lived through similar experiences. He says, "You never really understand a person until you consider things from his point of view. . . until you climb into his skin and walk around in it." Scout struggles with varying degrees of success to put Atticus's advice into practice and to live with sympathy and understanding towards others. At the end of the book, she succeeds in comprehending Boo's perspective.

- Teach specific types of writing in context. Each type of writing has its own conventions, most of which are not intuitive to students, especially those new to academic writing. Whether you are teaching them to write a persuasive essay or to write about how westward expansion changed the American landscape, you need to teach students how to write such texts. Here is an example of a handout I created to help students learn the conventions of writing a letter. In this case, students were writing a thank-you letter to Helen Farkas, a Holocaust survivor who had come to our class to speak about her experiences. This event provided a natural opportunity to teach them how to write such a letter while also giving me a way to tie together all that we had been learning prior to Mrs. Farkas's talk. Note that the example is designed to teach, not be a complete letter. After giving them a copy, I put the same document on the overhead and talked them through the points, asking them to draft their own as we went. Once they had working drafts, we went to the computer lab to type them up and revise them through conferences.

Sample Thank-You Letter and Format

Your letter should be:
- Properly formatted
- Specific, including examples from the visit
- Thoughtful and respectful in tone

400 Burlingame Way
Burlingame, CA 94010
September 24, 2007

> Sender's address and date at top

Mrs. Helen Farkas
1234 San Mateo Avenue
San Mateo, CA 94344

> Recipient's address

> Salutation: "Dear Mr./Mrs./Ms.?

Dear Mrs. Farkas:
Thank you for taking the time to come to our class to tell your story. Your story made me think about many things, but especially about how we treat each other. You and your family were abused not only by strangers but those from your own town. This made me realize, in a way I had not before, how degrading the Holocaust was for the Jewish people and others who were rounded up and taken away.

> Establish your purpose

One story you told made an especially strong impression on me... (choose one, summarize it, and explain why and how this one story affected you.)

> Double-space between paragraphs and do not indent.

Your story was filled with such pain and suffering, with so much loss, and yet when you finished you had only words of hope to offer us. I would assume that such an experience would leave one bitter—about everything! Yet you said, "No matter how bad today is, you always have tomorrow." Thank you for coming to our class, and for sharing your story with us.

> Restate your purpose near the end.

Sincerely,
Jim Burke

> End letter properly and sign your name.

- In the example that follows, I created a one-page handout intended to help students write analytically and revise the same document later. While preparing the assignment, I noticed that when writing about setting, for instance, effective analysis would require the use of certain verbs and nouns. Moreover, I realized that the analysis required a certain sentence structure. Thus I gave students this handout and, after working through it with them, had them apply it to their own writing, especially when revising. They had to highlight all their verbs and examine the structures of their sentences, revising as needed to achieve greater precision.

Analytical Writing

Analytical Verbs	Setting Adjectives	Setting Nouns
Establishes	Idyllic	Environment
Emphasizes	Pastoral	Era
Conveys	Chaotic	Atmosphere
Evokes	Alienating	Climate
Affects	Conservative	Region
Indicates	Divided	Background

Have students evaluate and revise their writing based on needs and insights.

Students need some kind of map that spells out where they are going and how to get there. On a writing assignment, this map is sometimes a rubric, but on other occasions it might be the prompt or some sort of outline the teacher provides, examples of which I will include below. Regardless of the form, students need some means of assessing their performance throughout these stages of the writing process. Spandel (2005) calls this approach "assess[ing] to learn," then argues, "You cannot rework writing unless you hear the problem with the text" (5). As they begin that first draft, students can, as Spandel says, "hear the problem" only if they have some criteria they can turn to. While good writing does not follow a recipe, we do nonetheless know what ingredients go into a strong piece of writing; if students also know what to include, they are more likely to feel some measure of control and arrive at a more delicious end result. Spandel sums up her vision of success as "students who can read their own writing and who know what to do to make it stronger" (5).

All the evaluation in the world will make no difference if students do not have the chance to revise their writing as they go along. Nor is it adequate to turn them loose with a rubric and expect a perfect result. Students need examples of what, for example, "a *meaningful* thesis looks like," ideally an array of examples so they get a sense of what they are trying to accomplish as they write or have some means of comparing their own thesis to the standard as they revise. How many examples or how frequently they need to evaluate their work depends on the complexity of the assignment and their level of mastery. In an advanced class, I might have students use samples of whole essays or portions (e.g., introductions, use of quotations) to evaluate their work throughout the composing process; in a college prep English class, on the other hand, I might provide more concrete evaluation tools like rubrics, checklists, or those which follow. Here are some specific examples to consider using with students as they draft or revise their papers:

- Rubrics, while not appropriate for all situations, offer detailed guidance as to the qualities of an effective paper. When given to students at the outset, rubrics help students stay on course and revise with greater precision. Here, for example, is a sample rubric from a school district which, for a district-wide writing assessment, adapted the rubric used for the state writing exam. Teachers can easily incorporate such a rubric into their class for other writing assignments. In my CP English classes, for example, we use the district rubric to assess and revise students' essays in the class.

Essay Rubric

4 The Essay

- Provides a *meaningful* thesis that addresses the writing task.
- Demonstrates a consistent tone and focus, and illustrates a *purposeful* control of organization.
- Provides a *variety* of sentence types and uses *precise, descriptive* language.

3 The Essay

- Provides a thesis that addresses the writing task.
- Demonstrates a consistent tone and focus; and illustrates a control of organization.
- May contain *some errors* in the conventions of the English language. (Errors do *not* interfere with the reader's understanding of the essay.)

2 The Essay

- Provides a thesis or main idea that attempts to address the writing task.
- Demonstrates an *inconsistent* tone and focus; illustrates *little, if any*, control of organization.
- May contain *several errors* in the conventions of the English language. (Errors *may* interfere with the reader's understanding of the essay.)

1 The Essay

- *May* provide a *weak* thesis or no thesis that is related to the writing task.
- Demonstrates a *lack of* tone or focus; illustrates **no** control of organization.
- May contain *serious errors* in the conventions of the English language. (Errors *may* interfere with the reader's understanding of the essay.)

- Scoring guides offer more targeted ways of guiding writers as they write and later, when they revise. They can be global, attending to larger aspects of, for example, a personal narrative, or they can focus on a more specific aspect such as introductions:

Introduction Evaluation Rubric

1 2 3 4 5   Establishes a compelling focus and a thesis that can be proven

1 2 3 4 5   Establishes your credibility to the reader

1 2 3 4 5   Every sentence serves a specific purpose: no fluff!

1 2 3 4 5   Connects the topic to your reader in a meaningful way

1 2 3 4 5   Conveys the importance of the topic

1 2 3 4 5   Implies or creates an organizational structure for the essay

1 2 3 4 5   Provides an effective transition at the end to subsequent divisions

1 2 3 4 5   Addresses the writing prompt (or shows clearly that it will do so)

Comments:

- Checklists offer very precise suggestions for how to write or revise the paper. At their worst, they run the risk of being a recipe that exerts too much control over the writer; however, they can be helpful, especially to those writers who are struggling to master these new, more complex forms of academic writing. I tend to use them more during revision. The following example is representative of what they look like and how I use them. In the middle of the writing process, I collected students' personal essays on an ally and read them through, scribbling down observations about those patterns of error or areas of need that were most common to all. When I returned the essays, I also gave them the following handout, which I discussed in detail with them, asking them to apply some of the items in class as we worked through the checklist. The more specific to an assignment a checklist is, the more useful it will be (from my actual class handout):

Allies Essay: Suggestions and Checklist

☐ **Titles:** Give your paper an interesting title (Hint: "Allies Essay" is *not* an interesting title). Here are examples which no one better use: My Uncle the Jedi Master... or Grandma's Cure....

☐ **Questions:** Ask the reporter's questions—who, what, when, where, why, and how—of everything. And ask the seventh, most useful but difficult question: *So what?* Or *who cares?* These questions help you explain why an experience is important, how it changed you, for example.

☐ **Revisit the prompt:** Some of you did not write about the prompt but sort of wrote around it. The prompt doesn't ask you to say what a great guy your uncle is; it asks you to tell the reader how he is your ally, what he does for you, how he has helped you solve problems.

☐ **Lights! Camera! Details!** Help the reader *see* and *hear* these wonderful people by adding dialogue, describing them, and generally showing them in action, *doing* these things you say they did to help you.

☐ **Be specific:** Try to avoid the word *thing* in your essay. Use concrete, specific nouns to help us see and understand what you are saying.

☐ **Avoid clichés or overused phrases:** In this essay, for example, many of you say repeatedly, "He was really there for me." Instead of "there for me," write, "He encouraged me, telling me he would support me no matter what I chose to do."

☐ **Examples:** Often you say these people helped you overcome obstacles but then don't give examples of what they *did* or what the obstacles were. Good writing has examples to help the reader see, hear, and understand what you are writing about.

- Templates are the most heavy-handed means of guiding and assessing students. While they are rarely appropriate for more advanced students, students who are still learning academic writing and conventions (e.g., English learners) find them very helpful, as do students who lack confidence in their own writing abilities. The following example was created by several colleagues in my department. They found this helped not only their college prep freshmen students but themselves, as it allowed them to articulate for their students and themselves what the paper should include and accomplish. I interviewed several students, asking them how helpful they found it; almost all students, especially those with identified learning differences, found it extremely helpful. Here is the template:

Of Mice and Men Outline

Throughout our study of John Steinbeck's *Of Mice and Men*, we have been discussing the question "Am I my brother's keeper?" and examining our responsibilities to other people. Through a class unit, we have analyzed the qualities of a good friend and critiqued the relationships between characters in the story. The purpose of this essay is to analyze George and Lennie's friendship and prove or disprove that George has the qualities of a good friend. Use the outline and examples from the text to support your ideas.

I. Introduction

- Did you mention the title, author, and basic plot of the novel?

- Did you discuss your general ideas about Lennie and George's friendship?

- Did you conclude your introduction with a statement of the specific qualities a good friend should have and explain that these are qualities that George does/does not have?

II. Body Paragraphs

- Did you begin each body paragraph with a topic sentence that presents a specific quality of a good friend and also indicate whether George has this quality?

- Did you use one or two quotations to support your discussion?

- Did you conclude each body paragraph with a concluding sentence that summarizes the paragraph?

III. Conclusion

- Did you begin your conclusion by mentioning the qualities of friendship?

- Did you then discuss how these qualities of a friend relate to your own life and your personal views?

Create opportunities for feedback throughout the drafting and revision process.

Writing is a social activity, done most often for an audience, even if that audience is sometimes the teacher. All writers need feedback from their readers or those who can help them to improve whatever they are writing. (There is, of course, no occasion to get such feedback when students write timed essays for you or some other audience such as the state.) Such opportunities provide students the chance, when working together, not only to get feedback on their own papers but to learn from others who are writing about the same topic, though perhaps in a different way. We often have severe time constraints, however, so feedback must be efficient if we are to find the time to do it, and effective if it is to be worth the time we allot for it. Perhaps the most important point to make about feedback is that it is only useful to

Noah Berger

the extent that students have the chance to apply it. If you return a paper with comments all over it which students cannot use to revise the paper, then they will look at it long enough to locate the grade and file it away. Thus the opportunities discussed here include two parts: the chance for students to get the feedback and the chance to put it to use to improve their performance on the paper at hand. To the extent that it results in improved learning and performance, feedback is the most important vehicle of writing instruction. Yes, it takes time; it also makes a difference, especially when the feedback is coupled with in-class instruction.

Jim Burke

Here are some forms of feedback that I have found to make a difference:

Written response is useful but only to a point. What is not helpful is a paper dripping red ink with every mistake marked. The most useful comments are written in a positive tone and make specific observations. For example, instead of saying, "Your paper has no details!" you might write in the margin, "An example here would really help me understand what you are saying," followed by an arrow that shows the exact spot to revise, or "Your strong verbs here make a real difference." Studies have found that specific compliments motivate students to try to repeat whatever earned the praise. Another useful approach to written feedback is to note significant errors throughout, and then list the errors at the top of the paper for easy reference. For example, I might notice that a paper lacks a clear subject in most of the sentences, so I would underline all the offenders and write at the top, "Clear subjects," which would allow me to follow up with an in-class conference about what that means. I can then combine written with personal feedback, but do so more efficiently as I now know what the problem is and have some examples to use for the personal mini-lesson that might take place at the student's desk.

Peer response taps into the social aspect of writing and students' natural desire to work together. The quality of peer response depends on how well you prepare them to read, discuss, and respond to a given writing assignment. Peer response can be effective, but you must set up specific guidelines and show them how you want them to work. For example, students often need more help developing their ideas by adding details, examples, and quotations. What I will do is use a sample paper from a previous assignment or one I created myself, copying this to a transparency so they can watch me as I demonstrate. I will stop and circle a passage, for example, and write in the margin, "Why did this happen?" or "What is an example of this?" Most of the time I try to limit their responses to just questions since the answer to the question will presumably improve the paper. I don't want comments; I want responses that lead to better writing. Before I turn them loose, we talk about the kind of language their questions should use, sometimes putting examples on the board (e.g., "What are you trying to say here?" "How does this example relate to your main idea in this paragraph?" or "Why did you include the quotation?").

Guided response is more of a full-class approach that asks students to provide specific feedback to themselves as directed by the teacher. Because I have classes of up to 35 students, this is a technique I use often and find effective. It has the added benefit of complementing mini-lessons and other classroom instruction I have given. For example, if students are working on quotations, as discussed above, I will have them get out three colors of highlighters or crayons as we focus on strong sentence subjects. I will then ask them to highlight the first seven words of each sentence in the paper and then to evaluate the quality of their subject. I will say, for example, "If those first seven words *are* your subject—that is, if you have one of those big long messy compound subjects—you need to work on making your subject more concise." This sequence sends them home or back to the writing workshop with specific (and colorful) feedback they can act on. In academic writing, which often requires quotations and examples, I almost always use guided response to have them identify the quotations. Even strong students often ask, "What if I didn't find any?" My response is a grin and, "Well, I guess that tells you what you need to go home and work on tonight, doesn't it, Kevin?"

Student-teacher conferences are important opportunities for feedback but very difficult to achieve if you have large classes. Still, they are possible if you plan ahead and make good use of the time. They need to be purposeful, not exploratory. Students come to conference with me either about comments I've already made on their papers (as mentioned above, I will list 2–3 items at the top of the page for quick reference in such conferences) or about a problem they are having and want me to help them solve. Such conversations can also take place right at the student's desk. When I return

papers they need to revise, I often just drop down on a knee and go over a few things on the spot. Although I have terrible handwriting, I have come to see it as an effective means of forcing students to seek me out for translation, which creates the opportunity to discuss the comment further. Such conferences are easiest to have when students are working in the computer lab, which we do periodically: I move around the room, monitoring progress, snooping. I can use the mouse to quickly highlight some sentence or other detail and talk about that within the context of their paper, helping them to draft or revise it on the spot.

General feedback comes during and after the writing process. General feedback is addressed to the whole class and is based on observations I have made during the drafting and revision process, or after having read and graded the papers. When I read papers, I keep a pad of paper handy. As I read the papers, I watch for patterns of success or trouble. If, for example, I see a trend toward using stronger verbs, something we may have been working on recently, I will jot that down and note some examples. When I finish the papers, I type up my observations—general comments about what I saw most people were doing well or need to improve—and put them on the overhead, using them as the basis for my feedback on the paper that is now finished. In addition, I always copy two or three examples, all strong, but each different in a useful way. Again, I will put these on the overhead and read them aloud, interrupting myself to comment on particular points to explain why I think a particular move is effective and how the writer did it so others can try it next time around.

Keep in Mind English language learners often need additional feedback about issues (e.g., spelling, mechanics, word choice) that are not as urgent for other students. Here are a few suggestions to consider when providing feedback to English language learners: Identify and praise their strengths and effort; show them through examples how to correct certain errors; identify patterns of error or serious errors, but only point out a couple to correct and explain; ask them to keep a list of common errors they make which they can check as they write and revise.

5. The Polishing and Publishing Processes

Correctness counts—and always should when it comes to academic or any other public writing. By this point in the process, the students have all worked so hard to make the papers worthy of others' eyes that it would be a shame to abandon them and their papers. Proofreading requires patience and commitment, because it is based on specialized knowledge about rules and conventions that many students do not know. Colleges throughout the country consistently cite such errors as their greatest concern when asked about students' writing abilities; *Standards for Success* (Center for Educational Policy, 2003), a major report that came from such inquiries, offers detailed college-level writing standards. What is noteworthy about this report is that the first seven of these standards focus on issues related to conventions and correctness. Certainly state writing exams, as well as the SAT, ACT, and AP exams kids take, all recognize that some errors are inevitable when students are writing timed essays; in such tests, the expectation is that errors will not be so prevalent as to impede the reader's ability to understand what the writer is saying. The motto of such tests is "reward the student for what they do well and don't punish them for what they do wrong"; yet clearly the College Board and other such agencies expect a certain level of proficiency, and they want those reading the tests to get the impression that, given the chance to revise, the student would recognize and repair the mistakes.

How then to actually teach students to make that final draft worthy of their name and some wider audience? A quick answer, one I have mentioned repeatedly, is that they must care about the work, seeing it as a public representation of themselves instead of just another assignment. Here then are some principles to help your students learn to care deeply about all aspects of their writing.

Guiding Principles

- Cultivate a community of writers who value correctness.
- Teach students to be strategic proofreaders.
- Provide opportunities to learn and apply knowledge of conventions.
- Publish, perform, post, or present.

Cultivate a community of writers who value correctness.

What we say when we talk about writing shapes our students' perceptions of and attitudes toward it. If we focus on informal writing, treating everything as little more than a journal entry, we create in students some false sense of security and confidence that the world outside destroys as soon as they venture beyond school. While we certainly must provide regular opportunities to write for more personal purposes and in less structured ways, we should also foster a classroom environment that validates the hard work formal writing demands. Such a culture of expectations is the result of the way you work with and speak about writing. If you treat it as something to check off, something to get done, your students will quickly pick up on this and feel no commitment to get the right word, to make sure all the sentences are parallel, and to ensure that all the punctuation is correct. Here are some representative ways to cultivate and maintain such a commitment to correctness in your class.

- Avoid making any statements that dismiss or otherwise undermine the importance of correctness in writing. While it is perfectly fine, important even, to say, "This is not the time to worry about spelling or grammar; we will work on that when you proofread later," it is not acceptable to say, "Don't worry about spelling, grammar, and that stuff!"

- Reinforce the value of correctness by bringing in articles that emphasize the difference such knowledge and skills make.

- Emphasize the importance of correctness by sharing your own efforts to achieve it. We all have trouble spots that trip us up as writers. I talk about my own challenges, words like *believe*, and grammatical structures such as correlative conjunctions, pointing out that I have had to learn to watch for these problems and always take time to fix them.

- Resist the desire, no matter how hilarious the errors might be, to read aloud or otherwise make public, student errors. Of course it is funny when a student writes, "This experience really lowered my self of steam," when he meant "self-esteem." But if we post such mistakes, our most vulnerable kids will feel unsafe in our class. Save such fun bloopers for the dinner table or lunchtime conversations with colleagues—but even then, don't reveal the student's name. Privately address the student about the malapropism.

- Post helpful rules and posters on the walls to which students can quickly refer. Ideally these posters would target specific patterns of error that you know are common to the class at that time. This might be the subject of a mini-lesson you recently taught and want to be able to refer to as students work on a paper.

Teach students to be strategic proofreaders.

Students must first learn what they are looking for, where to find it, and, if necessary, how to correct it. For example, if you are teaching students about the mechanics of quoting (e.g., how to format the quotation marks, the citation, the end punctuation), you must first teach them how to identify a quotation and what a complete and correct quotation includes. You must, as the saying goes, teach your students to fish so they can feed themselves; that is, they must learn the strategies needed to correct their own writing. Certainly some students have language disorders that make this a more difficult challenge for them; still, they need to learn those strategies specific to their own needs, something the special education department can often help you with. In their excellent book *Getting It Right: Fresh Approaches to Teaching Grammar, Usage, and Correctness*, Smith and Wilhelm (2007) offer a useful model for teaching students proofreading strategies. The following includes some of their suggestions as well as my own for teaching proofreading strategies.

- Focus on teaching students to use one convention or find one rule at a time, then show them (by modeling) how to find and correct that one type. Obvious examples would include teaching them about possessive apostrophes or the difference between *who* and *whom*, then having them search for and check each usage. Those conventions you teach, however, should be connected to the paper at hand, not random items they have not used in their papers.

- Limit the number of types of errors you teach or ask them to find and correct to no more than three, emphasizing those you have recently taught or know they have not yet mastered.

- Practice and refine these strategies by having students read not only their own papers but others' to look for those errors the writers themselves may have missed.

Jim Burke

- Direct students to look for and highlight conventions that are frequent errors. You could pick the most appropriate items from, for example, your state standards, Andrea Lunsford's "Top Twenty," or your own list. To address formatting titles properly, you might have your students go through and circle the title of any article, book, or poem, then review the rule and ask them to check and, if necessary, correct the format of their titles.

- Provide additional guidance to any English learners in your class as they often have specific patterns of error; to help these students, you might arrange to meet with your English learners as a group and ask them to check specific areas for possible errors, taking that opportunity to reiterate the rules and reasons for them. Some of the most common errors include the following:

  - Count or noncount noun error
  - Incorrect or missing article
  - Preposition error
  - Repeated subject
  - Wrong verb tense
  - Irregular verb errors

- Wrong verb form
- Wrong order of adjectives
- Incorrect word ending
- Incorrect use of plural or singular

Provide opportunities to learn and apply knowledge of conventions.

Every paper provides an authentic context (within the academic environment) to teach different content. As I discussed in an earlier chapter, teachers accomplish much more when they can address conventions appropriate to a paper students are working on. During the drafting and revising phases, you have abundant opportunities to give targeted mini-lessons on those conventions and grammatical rules appropriate to the assignment at hand. You may have taught your students, through sentence combining and mini-lessons, how and why to use adjective clauses or appositives, or some other more sophisticated structures. Now is the time to ensure that they punctuated them correctly and have all the right words in the right order in the actual paper. Thus, you have a new round of opportunities for teaching specific skills and knowledge in context, which students can then put to use on their current papers. Here are some ways to help students learn and apply their knowledge about conventions.

- Have students use a rubric for conventions to analyze their own writing, taking advantage of this context to review or teach, for example, end punctuation. See the Quick Style Guide at right.

- Create a style guide with specific information about how the paper should be formatted and certain elements (e.g., titles) in their paper should be handled. Below is a sample style guide I created for my AP English literature classes.

Quick Style Guide

The following guide addresses common questions regarding format and conventions for academic papers in English classes.

Manuscript Format

- Double-spaced (typed)
- 12-point black font (preferably a serif font)
  - Times New Roman is a serif font.
  - Helvetica is a *sans* serif font.
- Margins should be 1–1.25 inches wide on both sides
- Put the appropriate header information on the front page: name, period, date, teacher
- Put the page number in the top-right corner of each page; place this in the header

Titles

- *Italics*: books, magazines, CDs, television shows, movies, newspapers, plays, paintings; note: italics = underlining (in handwritten essays)
- "Quotation marks": individual articles, songs, poems, short fiction, essays, chapters, television episodes (compared to the series, which would be in italics)
- CAPITALIZATION: All nouns, pronouns, verbs, adjectives, adverbs, and the first and last words of titles of publications and other artistic works (consult style guidelines for handling prepositions)
  - *One Hundred Years of Solitude*
  - "A Very Old Man With Enormous Wings"

Citations

- Author cited in the lead-in:

  - Miller argues that the common man is also a suitable subject of tragedy (9).

  - Krutch claims that "Tragedy is not, then, as Aristotle said, the *imitation* of noble actions, for, indeed, no one knows what a *noble* action is" (2).

- Author not cited in the lead-in:

  - "Tragedy is not, then, as Aristotle said, the imitation of noble actions, for, indeed, no one knows what a noble action is" (Krutch 2).

Referring to an Author

- When referring to an author, use the full name (e.g., Ernest Hemingway) in the first sentence; after that, refer to the author only by last name (e.g., Hemingway).

Punctuation

- Quotations: The period and punctuation marks go inside the quotation marks:

  - "One day a man may just pick up and walk out," writes Amos Oz.

  - Oz begins his novel *A Perfect Peace* by saying, "One day a man may just pick up and walk out."

- Block quotations: Four or more lines of prose; three or more of poetry. Indent them one inch front left side. Do not include quotation marks. End passage with period, followed by parenthetical citation.

- Apostrophe: Used for possession.

  - Singular: poet's

  - Plural: poets'

  - Ending in s or *eez*: Add an apostrophe to make possessive: Sophocles' plays

- Provide specific mini-lessons on conventions, including in these lessons explicit instruction on, for example, the use of colons; follow these discrete lessons by practicing the conventions through guided instruction; then, finally, have students apply this new knowledge to their papers. During such a sequence, I circulate around the room to confer with students at their desks to be sure they are doing it correctly and clarifying the rules for them if they are not.

- Incorporate lessons on more advanced uses of conventions to show students how they can affect the meaning of a sentence or larger piece of writing. One example would be to include samples from professional writers using the dash to set off certain information for emphasis. Some formatting conventions, such as bulleted lists, represent changes in the nature of certain genres of writing; depending on the genre and purpose of the given paper, you might make time to provide a lesson on how, when, and why to use such lists as well as how to introduce and punctuate them.

- Require students to maintain a working list of particular writing errors and, on subsequent papers, use this as a guide to check whether they have addressed those challenges in the latest paper. As the year progresses, students can remove or add to this list various conventions they are learning to control. The list could also serve as the basis for writing conferences. When you meet with your students one on one or in small groups, reinforce the notion that they are responsible for learning and correcting these errors.

Publish, Perform, Post, or Present.

Students have never had more opportunities to make their ideas and performances public. Thanks to MySpace and Facebook, podcasts and YouTube, millions of students across America are publishing their music, videos, poetry, and fiction, as well as their art and opinions. Of course *some* of this "publishing" might borrow its collective title from Norman Mailer's early book *Advertisements for Myself,* and still some, thanks to their shocking content, may merit not so much titles as ratings similar to those that identify the adult content of movies. Students sometimes come into my class on Monday morning with a wild look in their eyes; when I ask if they are OK, these students say things like, "Oh, I'm fine, Mr. Burke. I worked on my MySpace page for, like, 20 hours this weekend." In this context, they are saying they worked like a magazine or Web publisher might, choosing and laying out photos, adding and revising written content, perhaps even uploading some video footage. As for more academic content, which might mean research papers or essays, speeches and other expository writing assignments, there is a wide range of ways to give audience to these writings. The reason to do so is obvious: Students are motivated to work harder when what they write will be read, heard, or seen by others. Here are some possible ways to give students' writing a real audience.

In class: Students can display their writing on designated spaces on the walls, perform their work before the class, and deliver it through either formal or informal presentations or speeches. The class can also publish student work in bound anthologies and magazines.

Online: Students can post their work to a class Web site, blog, or podcast. Many schools have restrictions on anything that involves publishing student work or images online, so be sure to check with your district regarding its policies.

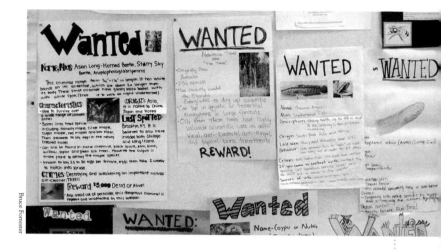

Around school: Students can publish their work on designated bulletin boards, in student publications such as the newspaper and literary magazine, and even in the school news programs broadcast to all classes. Obviously I don't suggest that all students read their essays to the school; still, certain assignments, such as an opinion piece, might lend themselves to in-school issues that would make a spot on the school news program appropriate for one or two students.

Through school: Most schools send out some form of newsletter; nearly all schools have their own Web sites; a few even provide more advanced forums like podcasts and television stations that broadcast over local cable stations. Depending on the type of assignment, some of these venues may offer rewarding opportunities to publish, if not the work of many students, at least perhaps excerpts from a few.

THE POLISHING AND PUBLISHING PROCESSES •

Beyond school: Writing contests are available to students; local and national speech contests provide annual competitions and other opportunities to speak. The "Laws of Life" essay contest (www.lawsoflife.org) is one in which many teachers in my English department have participated. It is an excellent experience, as it combines serious writing with meaningful recognition from an organization. At the same time, the essays themselves can double as wonderful speeches which the students can deliver in class or to another local organization that is sponsoring a speech contest. On a more informal level, students can find an audience outside of school—parents or other relatives, mentors— who can read and respond to their paper.

6. Assessing Student Writing

Writing assessment refers not only to evaluating a student's final paper and assigning it a grade, but also to measuring a student's knowledge of the elements of writing we have taught him. Assessment is a crucial part of the instructional process and of a student's growth as a writer, but it also demands much of the teacher. We might revise an old writer's saying to read that "we love everything about teaching writing except the paper work." Yet it is not true that we must assess everything students write; if we did so, our students would not write nearly as much as they must if they are to improve. Such purposeful writing requires a constructive response, feedback that helps students revise a specific paper and improve their future performance. Students themselves, however, must also reflect on their own writing and the strategies they use throughout the writing process, for if students do not internalize the writing strategies discussed throughout this book, they will not achieve the independence required to apply this knowledge in college or the workplace.

While we could frame writing assessment as both evaluating a paper and measuring knowledge of content (through an essay exam), this is not the place to discuss both in detail. Instead, coming as it does at the end of the chapters about the writing process, this chapter will examine how to evaluate and respond to a student's finished paper. In an earlier chapter on drafting and revising, I considered some aspects of assessing and responding to writers. Those remarks focused on the paper while it was being written; the student author then used the feedback to revise his paper. For the purposes of this chapter, assessment and response will concentrate on the completed paper, though this does not preclude the option of allowing students further opportunities to revise. Here then are the guiding principles for assessing, responding to, and reflecting on student writing.

Guiding Principles

- Use a variety of assessments.
- Respond to writers according to their individual needs.
- Invite students to reflect on the process, the product, and the performance.

Use a variety of assessments.

Every writing assignment exists within a larger instructional context. As the previous chapters illustrate, you are teaching students a range of skills, some of which culminate in a given assignment that, once polished and turned in, you must—choose your favorite word—grade, evaluate, assess, read, or score. While we use some of these words interchangeably, they do not mean the same thing. The word *assess* derives from the Latin *assidere*, meaning "to sit beside." This definition suggests more of a guiding role than a hard and fast score in the grade book. One gets the sense that to assess is to act like the master sitting down beside the apprentice at work to see how well he or she is learning the craft. Evaluation, however, requires that we interpret the results of a performance, in this case, a piece of writing. These results, which might be alternatively described as evidence of a student's learning, are the measure not only of their success but also of ours. Moreover, there is the dilemma of *what* to evaluate: the student's process or the content of the paper. As Calfee and Miller (2007) write, "We [cannot be] completely satisfied with our content and process labels. A contrast is also made between process and product, the differences between how a student writes a paper and the quality of the final work . . . . So we use *process* to refer to the student's activities in writing a composition as well as the characteristics of the written work" (273). That composition, however, is part of a larger body of work that can show progress over time more clearly than any one individual assignment.

Thus, when it comes to assessing the student's paper at the end of this process, the following approaches lead to improved writing over time if executed effectively.

Content and process grade: If you have been teaching specific aspects of writing (e.g., elements of argument, organizational patterns, use of supporting details, thesis statement) you can score papers for both content (i.e., students' mastery of the specific content you have taught) and process (i.e., the extent to which they followed the steps of the process for the assignment). This approach allows the teacher to hold students accountable for both the content and the writing without penalizing the student who is in the process of learning to use the strategies she is being taught. Content area teachers, moreover, can use this evaluation method to incorporate more writing in their classes without having to take full responsibility for providing explicit writing instruction if time does not permit it. In such cases, the social studies teacher, for example, can have students write an essay in which they explain the key factors that led to the Depression, simultaneously assessing their knowledge of the era and students' ability to assemble an effective historical argument, something most states include in their standards.

Rubric: Most of us must use one rubric or another: the state exit exam rubric, the AP essay rubric, a district writing assessment rubric (see example on page 75). So it makes sense to incorporate, when appropriate, the criteria by which our students will be evaluated. Still, rubrics have their limits: Some argue (Wilson, 2006) that they reduce writing to specific elements that do not necessarily constitute good writing. Moreover, these critics suggest that the harsh language that describes lower-level performance undermines the efforts of struggling writers who don't want to have their essay about their grandfather's struggle with cancer scored a "2" for its "lack of examples and sensory details, choppy sentences and grammatical errors." On the other hand, the obvious advantage of rubrics is that they provide specific information about what a successful paper will accomplish and save the teacher some time in evaluating the paper since the rubric provides a minimal but useful level of feedback. They also allow you to offer students specific criteria up front. Any state will have sample rubrics on its Department of Education Web site; these can be adapted to meet the needs of individual assignments. On the next page, I show the rubric I use in my Advanced Placement literature class, adapted from the AP literature exam rubric.

AP Essay Scoring Rubric

Score	Description
9–8 A+/A	☐ responds to the prompt clearly, directly, and fully ☐ approaches the text analytically ☐ supports a coherent thesis with evidence from the text ☐ explains how the evidence illustrates and reinforces its thesis ☐ employs subtlety in its use of the text and the writer's style is fluent and flexible ☐ has no mechanical and grammatical errors
7–6 A-/B+	☐ responds to the assignment clearly and directly but with less development than an 8–9 paper ☐ demonstrates a good understanding of the text ☐ supports its thesis with appropriate textual evidence ☐ analyzes key ideas but lacks the precision of an 8–9 essay ☐ uses the text to illustrate and support in ways that are competent but not subtle ☐ written in a way that is forceful and clear with few if any grammatical and mechanical errors
5 B	☐ addresses the assigned topic intelligently but does not answer it fully and specifically ☐ shows a good but general grasp of the text ☐ uses the text to frame an apt response to the prompt ☐ employs textual evidence sparingly or offers evidence without attaching it to the thesis ☐ written in a way that is clear and organized but may be somewhat mechanical ☐ marred by conspicuous grammatical and mechanical errors

4–3 B-/C	☐ fails in some important way to fulfill the demands of the prompt
	☐ does not address part of the assignment
	☐ provides no real textual support for its thesis
	☐ bases its analysis on a misreading of some part of the text
	☐ presents one or more incisive insights among others of less value
	☐ written in a way that is uneven in development with lapses in organization and clarity
	☐ underminded by serious and prevalent errors in grammar and mechanics
2–1 D/F	☐ combines two or more serious failures:
	☐ may not address the actual assignment
	☐ may indicate a serious misreading of the text (or suggest the student did not read it)
	☐ may not offer textual evidence
	☐ may use it in a way that suggests a failure to understand the text
	☐ may be unclear, badly written, or unacceptably brief
	☐ marked by egregious errors
	☐ written with great style but devoid of content (rare, but possible)

Comments

_____

_____

_____

_____

_____

Portfolios: More appropriate to the English class, I suspect, this approach emphasizes growth over time. Students write often throughout the course of the year, completing a range of papers on different subjects.

At certain junctures—the end of a grading period, for example—students choose a paper that represents where they are at that time as a writer and, if they have not already done so, revise and finish it before turning it in. In this way, students write much more, but the teacher does not have to read and respond to it all. This approach seeks to measure students' improvement over time as opposed to their performance on one specific assignment. Other teachers will score papers but also allow students to revise certain pieces in their portfolio and resubmit them, after writing a cover letter in which they reflect on their improvement, at the end of the semester for reevaluation.

The past semester, year, I wasn't always able to meet the requirements. But now I think I meet and exceeded the expectations. I didn't use to care on writing. I would just go in and try semi-hard. Though for this essay which was the first big essay of the year I tried. I prepared and I tried hard. That's such a great feeling to have when you tried hard and you get the grade that you earn. This essay I read the whole book, took notes, researched more than the book, and made an extensive outline which helped me out a lot because a lot of times I would get stressed out, but with the outline I didn't lose my train of thought and forget where I was in my writing. I just hope that in the future I can keep these strategies and will be able to get such high grades.

A student's reflection letter

Respond to writers according to their individual needs.

Responding to papers encompasses so many of the challenges of teaching writing successfully, all of which can be summed up by asking, "How can we respond to students' writing in ways that are fast but effective?" Correcting every error, writing detailed comments in the margin, offering encouraging and helpful summary remarks when we finish—these are noble goals, but if you have 170 (or more!) students, as many of us do, it's not possible. Well, that's not true; one of my colleagues worked with a teacher who kept an army cot in her classroom and, when she collected papers, spent the night in her room so she could return the papers to her students the next day. As a happily married man and father of three kids who strives for some measure of life-work balance, this is not a viable option for me. Our response to students' writing serves three main purposes: It provides guidance for revision of the current paper, it gives feedback students can use to improve their future performance, and it accounts for the grade you assign the paper. Here then are some ways to respond to papers when they are finished (as opposed to while they are in draft form).

- Avoid overfocusing on surface errors. Instead, narrow your remarks to emphasize the two or three most important errors, particularly those errors you have been addressing most recently through instruction. Look also for patterns of error, as these offer targeted opportunities for quick improvement.

- Show students alternatives to flawed usage or sentence construction. It's useless to tell them something is wrong if they have no idea how to do it right. For example, if a student writes, "World War Two was a very important war because it lasted a long time," when they were supposed to come up with a thesis about how the war changed American culture, you might scribble in the margin, "Jane, explain how it changed American culture. Ex: WW II galvanized

Americans, uniting them in a common cause to defeat Japan and Germany."

- Praise what they do well, making specific comments about their good work. Studies find that students make an effort to repeat what earned them praise. Thus, if you say, "The strong, active verbs in this paragraph really give your ideas power!" they will be more likely to focus on using strong verbs in future papers.

> At least 80 percent of my dirt biking experiences have been with Gary rooting for me or riding with me. Gary is a electrical engineer so he knows all about how things work and how to do the complicated electrical work that he teaches me.
>
> *how does this connect to the rest of ¶?*
>
> Ever since I have been a teenager, Gary has really made me feel more responsible and mature because of all the things he has taught me that no other kid at BHS knows how to do. He always works with me and does it my way until I mess up and he teaches me the right way to do that certain thing. If I ever mess up, he thinks it's a great learning opportunity and doesn't even gat a tad bit upset because he knows teenagers screw up a lot and they learn from their mistakes. Whenever we go camping together or go dirt biking, he wants me to learn how to dirt bike better so he will stop me and ask me to try and do something differently so I can improve my ability to ride over that terrain.
>
> *such as? · how? · why? · so?*
>
> *good! but be more specific*

- Avoid vague, general comments, as they are not useful. When you say that a sentence is "vague" or a paragraph "lacks focus," students tend to see this as your subjective opinion and dismiss it. Specific comments with explanation or illustration clarify what you are saying and help students see not only what to change but how to change it. Instead of saying a sentence is "awkward," for example, you might underline a part of the sentence and write, "How else to say this, Pat? I'm not sure what you mean here." In some cases, when it is quick and comes easy to you, you might write an example of how they might revise it to illustrate your point. (See example on page 101.)

- Respond like a reader (not like a judge), giving students your honest, supportive feedback as you read. When responding in this manner, your comments are more descriptive. I often write such notes as "Good idea in the ¶ but you lost me halfway through, Maria" or "I'm not sure how this relates to the previous paragraph, Dion." On some assignments, I might write at the bottom of the first page something like "After a whole page you still have not mentioned the book you are supposed to be analyzing. Consider revising to make the book the center of your paper." Such comments are best, of course, if students can then use them to revise.

 Keep in Mind Consider students' specific needs and development when responding to their writing. Advanced students often want more critical feedback. As one of my AP students said, "Tell me what I'm doing wrong and how to improve it. If I want praise, I'll have my mom read my paper." English learners, on the other hand, may want more detailed feedback on grammar, mechanics, and usage.

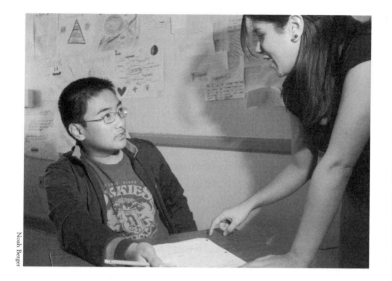

Noah Berger

Encourage students to reflect on the process, the product, and the performance.

As students use new strategies and learn new aspects of writing, they need the opportunity to examine the difference these strategies make. Each writer must study his or her own writing process, learning what works when, for example, they generate ideas. I have students who have learned that they need to talk their ideas through, so they schedule conferences with me during lunch to have a sit-down and hash out what they are thinking. Others need to just write, getting something down on paper no matter how bad. When the paper is finished and ready to be turned in, ask students to do some thinking about not only the final product but also their process and their performance. If they do not reflect, they will lack insight about how they reached the final result and will be unable to repeat what they did well due to a lack of awareness. Their success on a paper becomes an accident, something they cannot reclaim on future performances. Just as athletes watch videotapes of previous games, students should reread past essays. Here are some easy but effective ways to incorporate reflection into the writing process.

- Before they begin to write, students reflect on where they are in their development as writers, identifying those specific areas they need to focus on and the ways in which such an effort will improve their paper.

- During the writing process, have students pause to reflect, for example, on the questions they asked to help them generate ideas or write a particular section of a paper. They might also stop to reflect on what is not working and then brainstorm some possible strategies to help them solve that problem.

- After the writing process is complete and the paper is due, ask students to reflect on any of the following:

The strategies they used to write the paper. I tell students that I often don't know what I am trying to say until I write my conclusion, which then ends up working well as an introduction, at which point I cut and paste it to the front of the essay, tossing out the original introduction. Another strategy I often suggest, or even require, is to read each sentence and ask of it, "So what?" which has the effect of forcing students to explain the importance of their ideas.

Their performance on this paper in contrast to their previous papers, focusing on their growth and needs. An alternative is to have them reflect on their performance on this paper based on the criteria outlined on the rubric.

Their needs as a writer, reader, or thinker on future assignments. The most useful question is "What was hard and what went well?" Each assignment is a step in the year's long journey toward becoming a better writer, so it is important to keep asking where they are and what they need to learn to get where they want to be.

Recommended Resources and Readings

The following books proved essential in writing this book. They go into much more detail about the ideas I've discussed, as well as other interesting topics not touched upon in this book.

Alliance for Excellent Education (April 2007). "Making writing instruction a priority in America's middle and high schools." Washington, D.C. report.

Applebee, A. N., & Langer, J. A. (2006). *The state of writing intervention in America's schools: What existing data tell us.* Albany, NY: Center for English Learning and Achievement.

Booth, W. C., Columb, G. G., & Williams, J. M. (2003). *The craft of research.* Chicago, IL: University of Chicago.

Boscolo, P., & Gelati, C. (2007). "Best practices in promoting motivation for writing." In S. Graham, C. A. MacArthur, & J. Fitzgerald (Eds.), *Best practices in writing instruction* (pp. 202–220). New York: Guilford.

Burke, J. (2001). *Illuminating texts: How to teach students to read the world.* Portsmouth, NH: Heinemann.

Burke, J. (2002). *Tools for thought.* Portsmouth, NH: Heinemann.

College Board (2003). *The neglected R: The need for a writing revolution.* Report of the national commission on writing in America's schools and colleges. New York.

Connors, R., & Glenn, C. (1999). *The new St. Martin's guide to teaching writing.* Boston, MA: Bedford/St. Martin's.

Farrell, E. J. (1976). "The beginning begets: Making composition assignments." In R.L. Graves (Ed.), *Rhetoric and composition: A sourcebook for teachers* (pp. 220–224). Rochelle Park, NH: Hayden.

Graham, S., & Perin, D. (2007). *Writing next: Effective strategies to improve writing of adolescents in middle and high schools—A report to Carnegie Corporation of New York*. Washington, D.C.: Alliance for Excellent Education.

Graham, S., MacArthur, C. A., & Fitzgerald, J. (Eds). (2007) *Best practices in writing instruction*. New York: Guilford.

Hillocks, G. (2007). *Narrative writing: Learning a new model for teaching*. Portsmouth, NH: Heinemann.

Lanham, R. (2006). *The economics of attention: Style and substance in the age of information*. Chicago, IL: Chicago.

Levine, M. (2003). *The myth of laziness*. New York: Simon & Schuster.

Lindemann, E. (2001). *A rhetoric for writing teachers*. New York: Oxford.

Lunsford, A. (2008). *The St. Martin's handbook*. Boston, MA: Bedford/St. Martin's.

MacArthur, C. A., Graham, S., & Fitzgerald, J. (Eds.) (2006). *The handbook of writing research*. New York: Guilford.

Murray, D. (2004). *A writer teaches writing* (Rev. 2nd ed.). Boston, MA: Heinle.

National Council of Teachers of English (2004). *NCTE beliefs about the teaching of writing*. November.

National Writing Project & Nagin, C. (2006). *Because writing matters: Improving student writing in our schools*. San Francisco, CA: Jossey-Bass.

Smith, M. W., & Wilhelm, J. D. (2007). *Getting it right: Fresh approaches to teaching grammar, usage, and correctness*. New York: Scholastic.

Spandel, V. (2009). *Creating writers through 6-trait writing assessment and instruction*. Boston, MA: Pearson.

Wilson, M. (2006). *Rethinking rubrics in writing assessment*. Portsmouth, NH: Heinemann.